T0334102

Cambridge Elements ≡

Elements in Translation and Interpreting
edited by
Kirsten Malmkjær
University of Leicester

NAVIGATING THE WEB

A Qualitative Eye Tracking–Based Study of Translators' Web Search Behaviour

Claire Y Shih
University College London

CAMBRIDGE
UNIVERSITY PRESS

Shaftesbury Road, Cambridge CB2 8EA, United Kingdom

One Liberty Plaza, 20th Floor, New York, NY 10006, USA

477 Williamstown Road, Port Melbourne, VIC 3207, Australia

314–321, 3rd Floor, Plot 3, Splendor Forum, Jasola District Centre, New Delhi – 110025, India

103 Penang Road, #05–06/07, Visioncrest Commercial, Singapore 238467

Cambridge University Press is part of Cambridge University Press & Assessment, a department of the University of Cambridge.

We share the University's mission to contribute to society through the pursuit of education, learning and research at the highest international levels of excellence.

www.cambridge.org
Information on this title: www.cambridge.org/9781009114134

DOI: 10.1017/9781009122924

First published 2023

A catalogue record for this publication is available from the British Library.

ISBN 978-1-009-11413-4 Paperback
ISSN 2633-6480 (online)
ISSN 2633-6472 (print)

Additional resources for this publication at www.cambridge.org/Shih_pptx.

Navigating the Web

A Qualitative Eye Tracking–Based Study of Translators' Web Search Behaviour

Elements in Translation and Interpreting

DOI: 10.1017/9781009122924
First published online: March 2023

Claire Y Shih
University College London
Author for correspondence: Claire Y Shih, y.shih@ucl.ac.uk

Abstract: This Element reports an investigation of translators' use of web-based resources and search engines. The study adopted a qualitative eye tracking-based methodology utilising a combination of gaze replay and retrospective think aloud (RTA) to elicit data. The main contribution of this Element lies in presenting not only an alternative eye tracking methodology for investigating translators' web search behaviour but also a systematic approach to gauging the reasoning behind translators' highly complex and context-dependent interaction with search engines and the Web.

Keywords: eye tracking, qualitative research, retrospective think aloud, information behaviour, search engine

ISBNs: 9781009114134 (PB), 9781009122924 (OC)
ISSNs: 2633-6480 (online), 2633-6472 (print)

Contents

1 Introduction

Most people use the Web for all manners of information purposes at the present time. It is no coincidence that translators also rely heavily on the Web for information. A translator may choose not to use Computer-Assisted Translation (CAT) tools, but it is unlikely that they do not use the Web. In other words, web search is probably one of the most widespread and universal forms of Human Computer Interaction (HCI) for translators. Yet, unlike the use of CAT tools, translators' use of the Web is the least researched in translation studies so far.

The issue about the Web and search engines (presumably a gateway to the Web) is that they are not specifically designed for translators. It is not always straightforward for translators to find or locate what they intend to find. Frustrations of using the Web are not exclusive to translators though. In fact, it is found that many internet users cite the inability to find the information they seek as one of their frustrations of using the Web (Kobayashi and Takeda 2000: 146). It is largely a mystery why sometimes it is easy for translators to find what they are looking for and yet at other times it is almost impossible to find the information they need. The situation is even more complex when taking into account that modern search engines tend to automatically customise search results based on factors such as a user's geographical location, previous search queries and browsing history (see www.wordstream.com/serp). As a result, even when different translators share the same aim of finding the same information and using the same search engine, they can retrieve different search results (Shih 2019). A wealth of studies can be found in information science with respect to how humans acquire information (see Case and Given 2016). In particular, in search engine research many early attempts have been made to utilise search logs from search engine servers. For example, 'mean terms per query' (i.e. how many terms/words are used per query) have been found to range from 2.35 to 2.92 (Spink and Jansen 2004: 82–3). It has also been found that only one (search) results page is viewed in most search instances (Spink and Jansen 2004: 108–9). Researchers have also found that web users tend to follow an 'F shape reading pattern', that is, from left to right and from top to bottom (see Nielsen 2006) when viewing webpages. Such analysis provides interesting insights into web search trends or tendencies and indeed is very useful for search engine providers to improve their services. However, it falls short of distinguishing web search used in specific contexts and for specific purposes (Shih 2019: 911–12). This is why in recent years substantial research efforts have been directed towards examining the web search behaviour of specific user groups for specific tasks. For instance, many studies have focused on web search for health-related information, that is, the 'Dr Google' phenomenon (see Beutelspacher 2019; Kessler and Zillich 2019; Lee et al. 2015). Another popular theme is consumers' web search behaviour (see Hodkinson et al. 2000). A consensus that stands out from many of these studies is that information behaviour is highly complex and task dependent (see Aula et al. 2005; Byström and Jarvelin 1995; Granka et al. 2008; Marchionini 2006). This warrants detailed investigation into (web-based) information behaviour in translation.

These are some of the reasons that motivated me to produce this Element, which can be seen as a follow-up work to my previous three publications on translators' web search process (Shih 2017, 2019, 2021). It seeks not only to consolidate and confirm findings of existing studies, but also to add fresh empirical data so as to form a broader overview of the phenomenon of translators' web search. In other words, my aim is to demystify translators' use of the Web with a special focus on search engines, including queries, browsing and clicking behaviours, and the potential interplay among them.

The aims of this Element can be summarised into the following three themes and corresponding questions (see Table 1).

2 Existing Studies

Relevant literature and concepts in three research areas will be examined: Human Information Behaviour, Web Information Retrieval and Web Search in Translation Studies, as they will form a solid theoretical foundation in this Element. Section 2.1 'Human Information Behaviour' will explore the most prominent concepts and models of human information behaviour and how they may be adopted to understand translators' web search. Section 2.2 'Web Information Retrieval' will first focus on the basic mechanics behind search engines and then move on to important concepts and findings in this field. Section 2.3 'Web Search in Translation Studies' will present the latest and previous studies on web search in translation studies.

2.1 Human Information Behaviour: Theoretical Considerations

Human Information Interaction (HII) is considered by many scholars to be a sub-field of Human Computer Interaction (HCI), with a stronger emphasis on humans and less emphasis on computers (Jones et al. 2006). The term HII is coined to bring together all relevant studies dealing with how humans interact with information (disregarding which information systems are used) across many adjacent disciplines and sub-disciplines, including Information Retrieval (IR), Human Factors (HF) and Human Information Behaviour (HIB). More recently, Fidel (2012) simply calls HII a meta-discipline that encompasses studies dealing with humans, information and technology. While the boundaries

Table 1 Themes and corresponding questions.

Themes	Corresponding Questions
Translators' use of web-based resources	• What types of web-based resources are used by translators? • What types of web-based resources are used most frequently by translators and why? • How are web-based resources used by translators?
Translators' use of search engines I: query related	• What types of queries do translators use in search engines? • What types of queries are used most frequently by translators and why? • What does query intent entail? • How and in what circumstances do queries relate to query intent?
Translators' use of search engines II: browsing and clicking related	• What sequence or pattern of browsing and clicking behaviour takes place in translators' interaction with the search engine results page (SERP)? • When do translators decide not to click on any hyperlinks in the SERP and why? • What determines translators' clicking and browsing behaviour?

of HII may be fluid and subject to debate, given it is a relatively young (sub-) field, I consider that this Element largely falls into HII, and more specifically, HIB, the behavioural side of HII. This is because this Element depicts the behaviour of a specific type of information users, that is, translators, in how and why they interact with web-based information and systems.

Several terms and concepts in HIB are often cited in translation studies and its adjacent disciplines. They will be explained briefly in the following. These terms are: Information Behaviour (IB), Information Seeking Behaviour and Information Search Behaviour. Incidentally, even though these three concepts stem from HIB, they have been embraced and researched extensively in information and library studies (ILS). As a result, the most prominent IB models are developed within ILS. This is the reason why IB models from ILS will be featured in detail in this section later. According to Wilson (2000: 49), IB is an umbrella term referring to any behaviours that occur when humans encounter information sources and media. Such information sources do not have to be online. They can also include face-to-face interaction with another human being. In addition, HIB consists of both active information seeking and passive information reception (e.g. viewing advertisements online or on TV). In contrast to IB, Information Seeking Behaviour refers to purposeful information seeking. In other words, there must be a purpose or a need to search for information. Information need as a concept in Information Seeking Behaviour will be discussed later in this section as it has direct implications for translation. Finally, Information Search Behaviour refers to humans' micro-level behaviour with any information sources. These micro-levels include the physical level (such as moving the mouse to click on a link), the intellectual/strategic level (such as using Boolean symbols in search engines) and the mental level (such as judging which information sources are more relevant or reliable). To sum up, there is a hierarchy between these three concepts. Information Behaviour is a wider and more generic concept sitting at the top of the hierarchy, whereas Information Search Behaviour is at the lower end of the hierarchy, referring to lower-level details of the information behaviour. Most web search studies on translation adopt concepts from Information Seeking Behaviour, particularly the concept of 'information need', probably because of its saliency and ease of application to translation. After all, the information need or the purpose of information seeking in translation is largely self-explanatory; it is to solve problems encountered in translation. This problem-solving aspect also ties in seamlessly with translation process research (TPR). While it is important to recognise the theoretical and conceptual value of Information Seeking Behaviour in translation studies, this Element intends to go one step further in adopting the conceptualisation of Information Search Behaviour in addition to Information Seeking Behaviour. This is because Information Search Behaviour offers an ideal platform to dig deeper into the micro- or granulated level of translators' information behaviour, particularly in relation to their search engine behaviour involved in this process, such as clicking and browsing behaviour, strategic planning and judgement of relevance in information sources. This is part of the reason why the term 'web search' rather than 'information seeking' is used throughout this Element. In the following, several prominent IB models and theories will be presented, as they will help contextualise the phenomenon of translators' web search and inform the data analysis presented later in this Element.

Dervin's Sense-Making Theory (1983) is probably one of the most cited concepts in ILS and its adjacent disciplines. Dervin describes her Sense-Making Theory as not just a theory but also an approach or methodology for communication and information science. The three main components of Sense-Making Theory are situations, gaps and uses (Dervin 1983: 9). The situation is described as a context from which sense is constructed. The gap is a bridge that links the situation and the use; it is often referred to as the information need in the information-seeking literature. The use refers to the constructed sense or outcome (to be acted upon). Dervin believes that human reality is full of gaps (of information). When a human observes or identifies an information gap, they have an inherent urge to bridge the gap. Some scholars even call humans 'informavore' (Miller 1983). It is only when the gap has been filled that new knowledge is formed. Sense-Making Theory is often used to explain the fluid transition between information and knowledge. In other words, information is a relatively neutral set of codes and data. It can only become sense or knowledge once links are established and the gap is filled. In other words, the process of sense making is the process of transforming data or information into knowledge (by an individual). Sense-Making Theory is no doubt a useful theory to conceptualise the process of translators' web search because when translators resort to the Web for information, they are bombarded with huge amounts of information. It is vitally important for translators to 'sift out' relevant information and 'make sense' of it before they are able to adopt or use it in their translation. From this point of view, it can be said that this Element is partly aiming to portray the complexity of translators' sense-making process when faced with a magnitude of information on the Web. As mentioned earlier in this section, Dervin considers sense-making as not just a theory but also a methodology. In fact, to a certain extent, this Element also subscribes to the methodology of Sense-Making Theory epistemologically. Dervin (1998) describes sense-making as a 'verb', not a 'noun', as it is a continuous process. She explains that an important part of her Sense-Making Theory is to develop methodology to investigate what she calls the 'Micro-Moment Time-Line Interview'. This is because as the knowledge-forming process is continuous and ever-changing, partly due to its constantly shifting contexts/situations, it is essential to utilise micro-moment timelines so that the knowledge-forming process can actually be captured (in research). She proposes that in the data collection method (in her case, interview), it is important to capture at least two of the three components of sense-making, that is, the situation, the gap and the use. Again, while this Element adopts different data collection methods than Dervin's study, its use of qualitative eye tracking-based research methodology is essentially utilising empirical data to re-construct the situation, the gap and the use of translators' web search process at a 'micro-moment' level.

In the field of HII, several theories are widely cited and applied in search engine research, which are of particular interest in this Element. They will be examined here. One of the most renowned HII theories is Information Foraging Theory developed by Pirolli (2007). By drawing inspiration from Optimal Foraging Theory in biology and anthropology (Stephens and Krebs 1986, cf. Pirolli 2007), Pirolli cleverly uses several metaphors to explain how humans select and navigate the 'information maze' on the web. The first metaphor is that when an animal is foraging in a patch, over time the yield will gradually diminish. Eventually, it will be time for the animal to move on and look for a new patch. The tipping point of moving on to a new patch rests on the time cost between the energy it takes to search for food and the amount of energy the food can provide to sustain the animal. In other words, the time cost in the former must not surpass that of the latter for it to be worthwhile for the animal to stay in the same patch. This optimisation of cost and gain is readily applied in information studies. The patch is a website or webpage. A searcher will need to determine the balance between the cost (e.g. time and effort) it takes to find relevant information and the quality of the information gained (e.g. how relevant the information is). If the cost is much higher than the quality of information it provides, a searcher will move on to other information sources. The second metaphor is known as 'information scent'. This metaphor is used to explicate the judgement of how relevant the information really is. 'Information scent' basically comprises the 'proximal cues' of relevance a searcher picks up along the path of information seeking (Lewandowski and Kammerer 2021). In the case of search engines, the scent comes from URLs, titles and snippets (a summary or short description of the webpage content) attached to hyperlinks displayed in the search engine results page (SERP). The stronger the scent, the stronger the clues so that a searcher is more likely to click on a hyperlink. This behaviour is often accompanied by 'satisficing' behaviour. The word 'satisficing' merges two words, to 'satisfy' and to 'suffice'. It means 'to act in such a way as to satisfy the minimum requirements for achieving a particular result'.[1]

---

[1] See www.collinsdictionary.com/dictionary/english/satisfice.

In other words, a searcher may not evaluate all the search results available (based on information scent) but only evaluate a limited number of them until 'good enough' information is found. Notably, the rule of 'satisficing' becomes the gold standard for search engine ranking algorithms where sponsored links or the most relevant links are always placed at the top of the SERP, given it is proven in IR research that hyperlinks placed towards the bottom of a SERP are less likely to be browsed and clicked.

While Information Foraging Theory focuses more on the browsing behaviour in information seeking, a berrypicking model focuses more on query and its relationship with information need (Savolainen 2018). A berrypicking model is sometimes known as a type of exploratory or evolving search in IR research. Exploratory search is another important concept related to search engines, which will be discussed separately in Section 2.2.3. According to Bates (1989: 408), the classic IR model is not sufficient to explicate the complexity and dynamics of the information seeking process, as it assumes that the information seeking process starts from a single information need, resulting in a single query that matches a document representation and consequently a document is retrieved. Bates therefore proposes her berrypicking model, using the analogy of berrypicking in the woods to explicate the complexity of dynamics in the information seeking process. In this model, a searcher is like a berrypicker who has a general aim of picking berries in the woods. They have to pick one berry at a time and also find their way through the woods, as not all berries can be found in a single bush and berry bushes are scattered around different parts of the woods. In other words, as the searches go on, even though the overall aim has not changed, individual mini-aims have to be established and fulfilled. The searcher has to adopt a particular pathway in order to successfully pick enough berries. In Bates' own words (1989: 410):

> at each stage, with each different conception of the query, the user may identify useful information and references. In other words, the query is not satisfied by single final retrieved set, but by a series of selections of individual references and bits of information at each stage of the ever-modifying search. A bit-at-a-time retrieval of this sort is here called *berrypicking*.

The berrypicking model will be useful in conceptualising and understanding the lengthy and complex web search behaviour of translators in this Element, particularly in terms of the ever-changing dynamics of queries and query intents. Details and examples of these will be illustrated in Section 4.

In addition to Information Foraging Theory and the berrypicking model, Prominence-Interpretation Theory (Fogg 2003) also explains factors involved in the evaluation or judgement of how relevant information is. This is often called 'credibility judgement' (Kattenbeck and Elsweiler 2019) or 'credibility assessment' (Kammerer and Gerjets 2012). According to Fogg (2003), there are two components in this evaluation: prominence and interpretation. Prominence is defined as 'the likelihood that a website element will be noticed or perceived' (Fogg 2003: 722). Interpretation is understood as 'a person's own judgement about an element under examination' (Fogg 2003: 723). Fogg's theory is commonly used to explain how different elements or placement of information on websites may determine the information judgement. However, Kammerer and Gerjets (2014) adopt Fogg's theory to evaluate SERP, which is of particular relevance in this Element. According to Kammerer and Gerjets, prominence represents how salient the information clue is in the SERP, while interpretation represents a searcher's own idiosyncratic interpretation of this clue. In other words, the combination of how information is presented or formatted in the SERP and how a searcher makes sense of the information (cf. Dervin's Sense-Making Theory) ultimately determines how relevant or credible a SERP listing is. It is worth adding here that according to Fogg (2003), a searcher's own past experiences, long-term memory and even their knowledge about search engines may play an active role in contributing to their individual judgement and interpretation.

Another influential scholar in the field of information seeking is Kuhlthau (1990, 1991). Her most important contribution to the field is largely characterised by the introduction of affect in the understanding of the information seeking process. This incidentally coincides with the call for more emphasis on research about affect in translation studies alongside cognition and behaviour (Shih in press). In many ways, Kuhlthau's work can be considered to add to Dervin's (1983) Sense-Making Theory, in which sense-making is effectively a process of forming a personal view. The personal view formed by an information seeker cannot escape from their own affective experiences of everyday life. In other words, interactions are always present between the formalised information that an information seeker seeks and informal information derived from the information seeker's unique personal experience in life (Kuhlthau .1991: 361). After all, this is how an information seeker 'make(s) sense' of the world. Kuhlthau's work is also partially based on Kelly's (1963) personal construct theory, which depicts how affective experiences contribute to the way individuals construct knowledge and meaning. Particularly relevant to this Element is that this theory also highlights the situation where confusion and anxiety arise when newly sought information contradicts existing knowledge. Sometimes such confusion and anxiety become so intense that an information seeker may choose to interrupt or even abandon the whole information seeking process. A more effective alternative to abandonment, however, is to form a hypothesis to be tested (with further information) so that new meaning/knowledge can be constructed. In this Element, it will be interesting to observe how and potentially why translators confront and resolve the situation whereby formalised information sought on the Web (or via search engines) appears to contradict their existing knowledge based on their life experiences.

2.2 Web Information Retrieval

In contrast to Information Seeking Behaviour, 'information retrieval [commonly abbreviated as IR] is a discipline that deals with the representation, storage, organisation, and access to information items. The goal of information retrieval is to obtain information that might be useful or relevant to the user' (Ceri et al. 2013: 3). To a certain extent, IR studies are concerned with the technical side of information seeking, whereas Information Seeking Behaviour is concerned with the human side of the same story. While a large part of IR research is beyond the scope of this Element, it is helpful to have a broad overview of the basic 'mechanics' behind search engines, given that they will form part of the discussion in Section 4.

2.2.1 Search Engine Mechanics

Ceri and colleagues (2013: 74) illustrate the basic mechanics behind how a search engine is built in what they call 'the architecture of a web search engine'. According to them, there are two processes involved in search engines: a front-end process and a back-end process. The front-end process consists of two layers of processes: a user interface (UI) layer and a query layer. The query layer itself consists of three components: query parser, searcher and ranker. When a query is submitted in a search box in search engines, the front-end process begins. Initially, the query parser will be hard at work parsing and understanding the query. Then, the query parser sends its request to a searcher. The searcher will locate relevant information from its database. Once relevant information is located, it will be forwarded to a ranker so that information is ranked according to its degree of relevance and/or other pre-determined criteria. The ranked information can then be sent back to the UI for the end user. While the front-end process is initiated by an end user, there is also another (parallel) process in search engines that is constantly at work but not directly initiated by the end user. This parallel process is called a back-end process. The back-end process consists of two layers of processes: indexer and crawler. Crawler is essentially a computer program that constantly collects, analyses and updates information from the Web; the indexer is a computer program that processes and categorises information for optimal storage and retrieval once information is collected. It is vitally important for the back-end process to work behind the scenes parallel to the front-end process so that search engines can function effectively (providing up-to-date information) and efficiently (generating instantaneous search results).

2.2.2 The Concept of Relevance

Apart from the architecture of how search engines are built, another important concept in IR is the concept of relevance. In defining this concept, Ceri and colleagues (2013: 4) point out a fundamental dilemma for all IR systems, that is, 'the relevance of results is assessed relative to the information need, not the query'. In other words, there is a gap between how well search results serve their purpose for an information seeker and the information input obtained by the IR system (which is a query). Ceri and colleagues (2013) also highlight three unique properties for the concept of relevance, that is, relevance is subjective, dynamic and multifaceted. This dilemma reflects a real challenge for computer engineers to improve or build a better search engine, given the complex nature of relevance itself and the fact that relevance is not determined by a query (i.e. input in IR systems) but by a searcher's information need, which exists outside the system and is largely out of the control of IR systems. Essentially, it is a guessing game for the IR system to work out how well a searcher's information need is fulfilled.

2.2.3 Exploratory Search

As mentioned in the previous section, exploratory search is an important concept in search engine research. This is a phenomenon first proposed by Marchionini (2006), who notes that there are three types of search activities: look up, learn and investigate. Look up refers to the most basic search task that assumes a simple (fact-retrieval) query and a simple answer to the query. In other words, there is a highly specified question and a highly specific answer. The other two activities, however, represent a more complex type of search. Marchionini refers to them as 'exploratory search'. Exploratory search is 'defined as the situation in which the user starts from a not-so-well-defined information need and progressively discovers more on his need and on the available information to address it, with a mix of lookup, browsing, analysis, and exploration' (Bozzon et al. 2013: 642). White et al. (2008: 433) describe exploratory search as follows: 'in exploratory search people usually submit a tentative query to get them near relevant documents then explore the environment to better understand how to exploit it, selectively seeking and passively obtaining cues about where their next steps lie'. In other words, exploratory search is a constantly evolving process between queries and browsing and clicking behaviour. This is probably why it is found to be a particularly suited web search strategy in discovering difficult-to-find medical concepts and terminology in translation (Shih 2019). Shih also reveals that translation web search activities can either be a simple look up or an exploratory search, or a combination of both, although the simple look-up approach seems to dominate in students' web search process. In the remainder of this section, I will focus on existing literature about web search within translation studies.

2.3 Web Search in Translation Studies

Before diving into details of relevant literature, it is worth pointing out that there is currently no consensus in translation studies with regard to uniform terminology to describe the phenomena that this Element intends to investigate, that is, the way in which translators look for and interact with information on the Web. While it is generally agreed that information literacy is an essential component of translators' instrumental competence (see EMT 2017; Göpferich 2009; PACTE 2002, 2017; Shreve 2006), a myriad of terms is used to address translators' online information behaviour, including the use of electronic resources (Olalla-Soler 2018), the use of digital resources (Hvelplund 2017, 2019), online consultation processes (Cui and Zheng 2021a, 2021b), information (seeking) behaviour of online resources (Sycz-Opoń 2019, 2021), interaction between translators and online resources (Gough 2016), and the web search process (Enríquez Raído 2011, 2014; Shih 2017, 2019, 2021). Largely due to its link to the concept of 'information search behaviour' and proximity to search engine research (as pointed out in Section 2.1 and Section 2.2), the term 'web search' will be used in this Element to address this unique information phenomenon as it pertains to translators.

The literature about web search in translation will be reviewed in two groups: studies adopting a qualitative approach and studies adopting a quantitative approach, as these have direct implications for the methodology adopted in this Element, which will be explained in detail in Section 3, 'Methodology'.

2.3.1 Studies Adopting a Qualitative Approach

Web search in translation is first explored by Enríquez Raído (2011, 2014) in a multi-case study of six subjects in a pedagogical setting. The subjects are four student translators and two professional translators. Two translation/web search tasks (from Spanish into English) are conducted a week apart. The second task is designed to be more complex than the first task. The study adopts a combination of screen recording, online search reports (a type of self-reflective reports), pre-task questionnaires and post-task interviews as its methodology. Being a pioneering study, Enríquez Raído's work is significant in several ways. She is one of the earliest scholars to draw on theories and concepts from Information Seeking Behaviour and Information Retrieval systematically in translation studies. For instance, she describes 'information need' as a recognition of a need for information motivated by a translation problem and 'information goal' as the type of information required to fulfil the information need (Enríquez Raído 2014: 40). The link between the information need, the information goal and problem solving leads to a general categorisation of the information goal as either source text (ST) comprehension related or target text (TT) production related. In addition, one of the other significant contributions of Enríquez Raído's work is that it demonstrates a combination of different qualitative data collection methods as a valuable approach to investigating translators' web search process. In fact, many subsequent studies have followed in her footsteps by adopting a qualitative approach and utilising screen recording as a main data collection method.

Gough's (2016) PhD project represents one of the studies that adopts screen recording as a data collection method. The screen recording is preceded by a larger-scale survey. Gough's work features extensive profiling of subjects' individual attributes and characteristics in terms of online tools and resources used, how frequently these resources are used and what procedures or strategies are adopted in web search, and so on. In fact, Gough proposes two taxonomies in profiling translators' web search styles. One of them is called 'Resource Type User Typology' (Gough 2016: 193), which includes the categories: the Dictionary Enthusiast, the Mixed Type, the Parallel Text Fan and the Machine Translation (MT) Adopter. As the characterisations used in this typology suggest, some translators prefer to predominantly rely on web-based dictionaries, others on parallel texts and some even on machine translation. Gough's other taxonomy is called 'Typology of Translator Research Style', listing the Economical Translator, the Prolific Translator, the Understated Translator, the Explorative Translator and the Moderate Translator (Gough 2016: 214). A particularly noteworthy finding from Gough's second taxonomy is that 'the most represented category, the Economic Translator (characterised by low research volume, high research speed), covered half of the sample' (Gough 2016: 255). In other words, while different varieties and tendencies of web search styles exist among professional translators, around half of them tend to spend a minimal amount of time and efforts on web search. Gough cites effects of the 'Google Generation' (Rowlands et al. 2008, cf. Gough 2016: 33) as a possible reason behind this finding. In other words, translators tend to adopt speedy and flickering information behaviour when searching information on the Web.

Focusing on cultural-specific translation problems, Olalla-Soler (2018) investigates how translators (working from German to Spanish) at various stages of their competence and development may use web-based resources differently. Her subject population includes first, second, third and fourth-year undergraduate translation students and professional translators. Like many previous studies, her main data collection method is screen recording. The main findings show that student translators generally spend more time on web-based resources and pose more queries in search engines in order to solve their cultural-specific translation problems. Professional translators, however, are found to spend less time on the Web and instead rely more on their own internalised knowledge in order to solve the problems (Olalla-Soler 2019). In addition, Olalla-Soler also points out that the whole student cohort behaves relatively similarly in their web search process. In other words, their levels and years of translation training appear to have no noticeable effects on their web search process. While it is understandable that professionals are likely to have more cultural knowledge to resort to when compared with student translators, it is interesting to find that years of training have no effects on the web search process in the student cohort. This may be an indication that web search skills represent an independent sub-skill that requires specific training, which current translation curricula may not have yet catered for.

Studies adopting the qualitative approach also include my two previous studies (Shih 2017, 2019) where screen recording and think-aloud protocols are used to elicit relevant data. The 2017 study is exploratory in depicting what types of web-based resources are used by student translators (working from English into Chinese) and their idiosyncratic web search behaviour, particularly in terms of queries used in different search engines (i.e. Google and Baidu). In common with many previous studies, it confirms that online dictionaries and search engines are the web-based resources most used by Chinese student translators. The 2019 study adjusts its focus to investigate optimised (i.e. effective and efficient) behaviour of student translators by adopting White's (2016: 21–37) concepts of primary action and secondary actions. Primary action refers to query-related actions in search engines and secondary actions refer to the actions conducted as a result of search engines but largely occurring outside search engines (e.g. how many hyperlinks are clicked and consequently how long translators spend browsing external webpages). The main findings indicate that 'exploring and processing a search engine result page at a deeper level can be a [more] effective strategy to satisfy a rare information need[/goal], particularly in the context of harder-to-reach TL terms. There [is] little evidence, however, to suggest that extensive query re-formulation alone makes much impact to the success of web search' (Shih 2019: 921). In other words, the key to successful and optimised web search (in search engines) lies in secondary actions (i.e. clicking and browsing behaviour beyond queries) and an exploratory search approach is more advantageous than extensive query reformulation in helping student translators to solve their translation problems.

A recent study that largely adopts the qualitative approach is conducted by Sycz-Opoń (2021). It is worth noting here that the methodology adopted in this particular study relies on direct observation and think-aloud protocols in addition to screen recording. Sycz-Opoń's student translators are instructed to work in pairs. One student acts as the recorder and the other student acts as the translator. The recording student is responsible for writing down details of the direct observation by using the 'observation protocol' consisting of a list of questions, for example, what web-based resources are used, why they are used, what information is being sought and the end result of the search. The translator is responsible for translating a legal text from Polish into English while thinking aloud. Sycz-Opoń (2021: 138–9) states that the translator is instructed to explain aspects such as their choices of information sources used, reasons for their decisions and quality of information sources used. The whole data collection process (n=104; 52 pairs) takes place in a single sitting in a computer lab where students are briefed for ten minutes and spend up to one hour and twenty minutes on the task itself. A taxonomy of six research styles is proposed based on the data: the Traditionalist, the Digital Native, the Minimalist, the Detective, the Habitual Doubter and the Procrastinator. While Sycz-Opoń's study reveals some interesting varieties of student translators' tendencies, her data collection procedures are not without potential flaws. Firstly, only ten minutes are spent in briefing the whole cohort of 104 students. This shows that neither the recording students nor the student translators have much time to practise or rehearse what they are supposed to do. Given that think aloud does not come naturally for most people, particularly while performing a complex task, it is worrying that the student translators are not trained in how to think aloud well in advance. This is aggravated by the issue that the student translators are instructed 'to explain their choices and decisions and comment on the quality of consulted sources when asked by the recorder' (Sycz-Opoń 2021: 138–9). In other words, the recording students are not only expected to write down many different types of information and behaviour, but they are also instructed to interrupt and pose questions to the student translators so that they could record the translator's explanations and comments. Alarmingly, this reveals that differences between think-aloud protocols and descriptions or explanations of one's thinking appear to be misunderstood (see Ericsson and Simon 1998). As a result, the findings of this study should be treated with extra caution.

2.3.2 Studies Adopting a Quantitative Approach

Web search related studies adopting a quantitative approach in translation all uniformly employ eye tracking as their main data collection method. Hvelplund, a veteran in eye tracking research in translation (see Hvelplund 2017: 248–64), is one of first scholars to investigate web search quantitatively (Hvelplund 2017, 2019). His 2017 study focuses on examining the types of digital resources being used by professional translators and the amount of time and cognitive load spent on drafting, revision and using digital resources, respectively. The subject population consists of eighteen professional translators working from English into Danish, translating two texts: a literary text and a Language for Specific Purposes (LSP) text. Keylogging, eye tracking and screen recording are used as data collection methods. In terms of the types of web-based resources used, unsurprisingly, bilingual dictionaries and search engines are found to be the most frequently used. In terms of time, using digital resources accounts for around 20 per cent of the total translation process. In terms of effort (by analysing eye tracking metrics, i.e. fixation duration and pupil size), the study shows that using digital resources requires significantly higher processing and cognitive load than drafting and revision. All these findings suggest that using digital resources represents a significant part of the translation process that warrants further investigation. Hvelplund's 2019 article draws on the same data set as his 2017 publication. This time he focuses on transition patterns between the ST, TT and digital resources, which he refers to as 'processing flow[s]'. One thing worth pointing out here is that the reason Hvelplund is able to use eye tracking algorithms to study the transition patterns between ST, TT and digital resources is that in his experimental design, he artificially divides the screen into three parts: keylogging software (i.e. Translog II) is on the left, which consists of two panes, the ST pane at the top and the TT pane at the bottom. The right-hand side of the screen is the web browser. As a result, the eye tracker is able to compute all screen-based activities that occur within the boundary of the top left-hand pane as ST behaviour; that occurring within the boundary of the bottom left-hand pane as TT behaviour; and that occurring at the right-hand side of the screen as digital resource behaviour. This exact experimental setup is taken up by Cui and Zheng (2021a, 2021b), whose study will be discussed later. Hvelplund shows that there are four different types of processing flows. Type 1 is source text to digital resources and back to source text, abbreviated as ST-DR-ST. Type 2 is source text to digital resources and then to target text (ST-DR-TT). Type 3 is target text to digital resources and to source text (TT-DR-ST). Finally, Type 4 is target text to digital resources and target text (TT-DR-TT). He indicates that Type 2 and Type 4 are not only the most frequently occurring but also the most (cognitively) intensive processing flows. He therefore concludes that the use of digital resources plays a substantial part in both initial drafting (Type 2 processing flow) and later revision (Type 4 processing flow) in the translation process

Focusing on translation directionality (i.e. from L1 to L2 and L2 to L1), Whyatt and colleagues (2021) also adopt a largely quantitative approach in their study. Like Hvelplund, they also employ keylogging, screen recording and eye tracking as their data collection methods. Their main findings suggest that compared with translation into L1, translation into L2 increases the intensity of temporal and cognitive loads in web search. In other words, translation into L2 takes longer and requires more effort in the web search process. Nevertheless, there is very little evidence to suggest that translation directionality influences the way in which translators conduct web search. Similarly, the amount of time spent on web search does not seem to have much correlation to translation quality.

Cui and Zheng (2021a, 2021b) are the latest researchers to take up eye tracking in investigating web search in translation. As in previous studies, keylogging, eye tracking and interviews are used as their main data collection methods. As mentioned briefly in the previous paragraph, they largely follow Hvelplund's experimental setup in dividing the screen into three parts. Thirty-eight postgraduate student translators are asked to translate two texts, one being an easier and the other a more difficult text. As in most previous studies, they find that the most used web-based resources are bilingual dictionaries and search engines. Unsurprisingly, the more difficult the text is (as perceived by translators), the more time is spent on web search. Similarly, more frequent and intense transitions between the translation pane and the web search pane could be found in translating the more difficult text. However, statistically, cognitive efforts do not correlate with translators' perceived difficulty. It is conceded that cognitive efforts may be linked to the types of problems encountered by each individual translator rather than the general perception of text difficulty. For instance, it is found that searching for extra-linguistic information tends to require more cognitive effort. In terms of the cognitive efforts involved in web search, Cui and Zheng (2021b: 68) suggest that a pedagogical implication can be drawn from their findings, whereby student translators 'should be given designated training in improving their working memory capacity', as frequent transition between the translation and the Web is a sign that student translators are struggling to cope with information overload. Interestingly, this point is directly related to a finding of the present Element and will be raised again in Section 4.

3 Methodology

This section will first elucidate a qualitative approach to eye tracking and then explain the rationale and significance of this methodology outside translation studies, particularly in usability research. Finally, the data collection procedures adopted for this Element will be illustrated.

3.1 A Qualitative Approach to Eye Tracking

Eye tracking is by no means new in translation studies. A quick search of 'eye tracking' as a keyword in the Translation Studies Bibliography, a specialist database for research publications in translation studies, generates hundreds of results. As a data collection method, eye tracking is first borrowed from cognitive psychology by O'Brien (2006) to investigate translators' use of CAT tools, that is, Trados Translators Workbench, an earlier version of SDL Trados Studio. In fact, O'Brien (2013) herself calls TPR scholars 'the borrowers', as they have consistently stepped out of their comfort zone, looked further afield from the traditional boundary of translation studies, and cultivated new research methods from other disciplines. This is likely to be the reason why TPR remains one of the most interdisciplinary areas of translation studies to date.

Eye tracking is used to investigate many different aspects of translation. From the late 1990s to early 2000s, researchers such as Michael Carl, Moritz Schaeffer and Arnt Lykke Jakobsen, originally based at the Center for Research and Innovation in Translation and Translation Technology (CRITT), Copenhagen Business School, pioneer the use of Translog, keylogging software in combination with an eye tracker. This develops into a distinct methodology using inferential statistics in its analysis. Since then, there has been a steady stream of publications using the same CRITT methodology (see Carl et al. 2016).[2]

While it is common to supplement the use of eye-tracking metrics with other qualitative data, such as screen recording, questionnaires or retrospective interviews (Saldanha and O'Brien 2014: 109–10), epistemologically, eye-tracking methodology has largely adopted a quantitative and deductive approach since it is first introduced to translation studies by O'Brien two decades ago (Saldanha and O'Brien 2014: 144). It is true that even outside translation studies, the gold standard for eye tracking data analysis seems to be primarily numerical and statistical. Some scholars even argue that visualised data, such as scan paths, heat maps and gaze replays, cannot be considered eye tracking data at all, and that only 'rigorous statistical analysis should . . . form

---

[2] While CRITT methodology was originally known to be quantitative and statistical, it is important to point out that over time such a research orientation can change when the amount of hypothesis-testing data reach a stage of 'saturation'. As shown in Carl and Schaeffer's (2018) study, by integrating a sufficient amount of data in different language combinations and studies, multiple hypotheses can then be generated using a grounded theory method. Hence, a quantitative research paradigm is 'metamorphosised' into a qualitative one.

the bedrock of [eye tracking] research' (Conklin et al. 2018: 208). A positivist and quantitative approach to eye tracking has many merits and indeed has made a significant contribution to translation studies and beyond. It is clearly advantageous in providing solid statistical evidence to advance the scientific investigation of translators' and interpreters' cognitive efforts in specific settings and conditions. Nonetheless, this approach also has its limitations. '[Quantitative] procedures are deductive in nature, contributing to the scientific knowledge base by theory testing. This is the nature of quantitative methodology. Because true experimental designs require tightly controlled conditions, the richness and depth of meaning for participants may be sacrificed. As a validity concern, this may be a limitation of quantitative designs' (Glenn 2010: 103). In translation studies, such controlled conditions can range from deliberate manipulation of STs and their length, to how and where STs are presented on the computer screen. All these controls and manipulations are designed to ensure the integrity of this type of research. Nevertheless, such control can also compromise ecological validity. In other words, the experimental setting and conditions can fall short of being realistic and naturalistic. In addition, findings generated from hypothesis-testing studies sometimes have limited direct applicability to translation practice. Typical hypotheses include whether variable A is linked to variable B, or whether variable A is a (probable) cause of variable B. Moreover, researchers are often called on to design experiments and hypotheses around specific statistical methods so as to avoid subsequent difficulty in analysing non-standardised quantitative data in eye tracking (Holmqvist et al. 2011: 108).

At this point, it may be useful to clarify what eye trackers can offer and perhaps more importantly what they cannot offer. Despite an abundance of measurements and promising results, eye trackers are fundamentally designed to collect two types of data: spatial data and temporal data of visual attention. In the plainest terms, eye trackers track where the eyes look and for how long; nothing else. What eye trackers cannot offer, however, some may argue critically, are the very reasons why such visual attention occurs. This inherent delimitation is one of the most crucial considerations of using eye tracking as a (main) data collection method. If a researcher is more interested in (acute) reasons behind translators' real-time cognitive efforts and behaviours, as in the case of this Element, eye tracking as a main data collection method is automatically discounted and should not be considered. Or so I was told . . . until I dived into usability studies, a sub-field of Human Computer Interaction (HCI), and its extensive use of qualitative eye tracking-based methodology. I discovered that a qualitative approach to eye tracking is not only possible but also proven to be valuable in its own right. Usability will be discussed in detail in Section 3.2.

As shown in Section 2, research into translators' use of the Web in translation studies to date can be divided into two methodological camps. The first one adopts screen recording as a main data collection method. In these studies, screen recording is often supplemented by translators' own retrospection, with the use of post-task questionnaires, interviews and self-reflective web search reports (see Enríquez Raído 2014; Gough 2016; Olalla-Soler 2018; Shih 2017). The methodology of these studies is purely qualitative in nature. More recently, however, a new type of web search study has emerged. These studies enlist eye tracking as a main data collection method, subscribing to a quantitative and hypothesis-testing approach. Meanwhile, they are also supplemented by some form of retrospective reports, including questionnaires and interviews, but often as secondary data to support the findings and hypotheses of the primary quantitative metrics produced by eye trackers (see Cui and Zheng 2021a, 2021b; Hvelplund 2017, 2019).

In distinction to other existing studies on translators' web search, the methodology adopted in this Element takes a qualitative eye tracking-based approach. It attempts to reconcile the methodology used by the aforementioned two camps of studies. On the one hand, eye tracking is employed as a means to record the real-time representation of translators' web search behaviour. On the other hand, the eye tracking recording is then used to prompt or cue translators to think aloud based on their real-time behaviour. In this way, synchronous and asynchronous data are brought together. At an operational level, this methodology optimally utilises gaze replay, a common function of visualisation in eye tracking software. The gaze replay, as the name suggests, is a video recording of participants' real-time gaze or eye movements. In other words, while translators conduct their web search and translation task, their eye movements are recorded on the screen in real time. This screen recording (with translators' eye movements being superimposed on the screen) is not only used as a type of raw qualitative data for detailed analysis but also as real-time and targeted cues to prompt translators to report on their web search behaviours immediately after they complete their translation and web search task. There are multiple advantages to this two-stage data collection method. Firstly, the gaze replay provides visualised data that are far richer and more precise than a traditional screen recording of translators' web search behaviour. Secondly, the qualitative cue-based retrospective report (i.e. retrospective think aloud) provides detailed inferences that greatly enhance our understanding of specific aspects of translators' real-time behaviour (i.e. query, browsing and clicking behaviours), which a quantitative approach simply cannot achieve. More importantly, a combination of these two datasets can offer a powerful insight into the interplay between different features of web search behaviour and translators' reasoning behind such behaviour, and potentially how emotive factors may play a role in web search. At this point, it is important to clarify that I am not claiming that cue-based retrospective interviews have never been used in translation studies before. In fact, they have been used in previous studies for some time. For example, Ehrensberger-Dow and Perrin (2009) replay screen-recording videos as cues to interview their student and professional translators. More recently, Guerberof et al. (2021) also use cue-based retrospective interviews to supplement their quantitative analysis to investigate cognitive loads of the UI in Microsoft Word.

Here, I would like to reiterate the main reasons why in this Element I decide to go against the flow and challenge the mainstream eye tracking methodology regularly employed in translation studies. First of all, relatively little is known about translators' web search behaviour. It makes sense to employ a qualitative and grounded theory approach to generate hypotheses so that such hypotheses can be tested in future research. In addition, this Element aims to establish when, how and why translators navigate their way through the Web. In other words, uncovering and modelling naturalistic web search behaviour is a top priority. A further reason is that while maintaining maximum ecological validity, it is operationally challenging to generate quantitative eye tracking metrics. Previous eye tracking studies in translation have imposed strict experimental manipulation and control over their translation tasks. Their ecological validity can suffer as a result. Part of the reason that these strict experimental controls are in place is linked to how quantitative metrics are generated in eye tracking research. The quantitative metrics in eye trackers are essentially computed from identical stimuli among different participants. Stimuli refer to what is presented on the computer screen that prompts participants to conduct or perform a task. In eye tracking experiments, stimuli act as crucial points of references. Without them, eye tracking metrics are pointless. In the case of translation, stimuli are normally a piece of ST, TT and its associated instruction presented on the computer screen. The ST is normally presented either at the top of the screen or on the left of the screen, and the TT is presented either at the bottom or at the right of the screen. In other words, fixed contents are placed in fixed locations on the screen as stimuli. However, unlike previous eye tracking experiments, I am not interested in translators' visual attention to the ST nor its corresponding TT. Instead, I am interested in the dynamics and patterns of translators' visual attention on different varieties of web-based resources and search engines of their choice. In other words, it is imperative that each translator does not just have complete freedom to choose which web browsers or web-based resources to use and what to do with them, but also where to place their chosen web browser or web-based resources on the computer screen in relation to their ST and TT. As a result, there is little identical stimulus or meaningful part of the screen among different translators for eye trackers to generate aggregated metrics. To mitigate this operational dilemma, I have two options. One is to abandon the idea of maximum ecological validity and create an artificial WWW environment, possibly with a staged search engine and several staged SERPs, so that points of references can be established; this would mean changing my research design and research questions for the sake of generating quantitative data in eye trackers. Or alternatively, I could retain my original research questions and design, and focus solely on the rich qualitative data that eye trackers and retrospective think aloud can offer. Clearly, I opt for the latter in this Element.

A final reason for choosing a qualitative approach is that as the aims of this Element are principally in line with usability in the field of HCI, that is, translators' interaction with the web and search engines, it is legitimate and logical to adopt a 'tried and tested' data collection method routinely used in usability studies. More details about usability will be offered in the following section.

3.2 Usability in Human Computer Interaction

Human Computer Interaction (HCI) is a multidisciplinary field that sits at the intersection between computer science, psychology, behavioural science, engineering, design, and so on. As the term literally suggests, HCI aims to study the interaction between human and computer. According to Hartson and Hix (1989: 8),

> the terms "human-computer dialogue" and "human-computer interface" (also called the "user interface") are defined separately to denote, respectively, the communication between a human user and a computer system and the medium for that communication. Thus, a dialogue is the observable two-way exchange of symbols and actions between human and computer, whereas an interface is the supporting software and the hardware through which this exchange occurs.

It is worth pointing out here that the software and hardware referred to above are not just restricted to supported computer applications, but also include any medium or techniques that enable the exchange to take place. Taking a simple action of typing on a keyboard as an example, according to Marsh (1990: 16–17), when a human types a lower-case 'a' on a keyboard, the letter 'a' is a code that human and computer use in their communication, whereas the finger pressing the letter 'a' on the keyboard represents the medium to carry out this interaction. In other words, the letter 'a' represents the dialogue, and the finger along with the keyboard (i.e. ergonomic aspects) represent the interface. This definition has acute implications for this Element, as the two HCI components, dialogue and interface, provide a very useful theoretical framework to understand web search behaviour. In fact, these two components are found to somewhat overlap with White's (2016) concept of primary action and secondary action regarding the use of a search engine, as discussed in Section 2. Obviously, the concept of dialogue and interface in HCI is much broader in its scope than White's primary and secondary action for search engines, given that the use of a search engine is only one type of human and computer interaction. As stated in Section 1, a detailed investigation of translators' interaction with search engines is of paramount importance because search engines are among the most frequently used web-based computer applications by translators. When a translator types a query inside a search box in a search engine, this query is a code or 'dialogue' being initiated by a translator with a computer. The web browsers and search engines are the 'interface(s)' to facilitate this exchange. The search engine responds to the query or replies to the dialogue by retrieving a list of SERPs. In other words, both the query and the SERP are the observable two-way dialogues between human and computer. Translators' subsequent mouse-clicking actions in the SERP represent the interface during this interaction. To a certain extent, the dialogue and interface tell the human side of the story of this human and computer interaction (Marsh 1990: 17). The computer side of the story, however, is related to underlying algorithms built for each search engine, which are largely out of the scope of this Element (see Section 2.2). In other words, what this Element aims to do is to illustrate the translators' side of the story when they interact with search engines and other web-based resources.

Of course, HCI is not a brand-new concept in translation studies. In her paper, titled, 'Translation as a human computer interaction', O'Brien (2012) first intro-duces the following two concepts into translation studies: 'human factors' and 'cognitive ergonomics'. According to her, the former refers to 'how people interact with tools and technology' and the latter is a more specific concept that is concerned with 'cognitive demands placed on users by the design and complexity of computer programs' (O'Brien 2012: 103). Interestingly, O'Brien's brief explanation about human factors and ergonomics seems to reveal that she merges two types of perspectives in the term human factors in HCI. On the one hand, human factors are considered to be a broad concept that is concerned with humans' use of equipment (not necessarily computer equipment), limitation of equipment designs, functions and performance, and of course how equipment can be improved for optimised human usage, and so on. In fact, in the field of HCI, human factors and ergonomics are considered to be the same discipline and are often used interchangeably.[3] This is probably why O'Brien (2012: 101) calls for 'a more caring and inclusive approach towards the translators by developers of translation

---

[3] See https://psychology.rice.edu/what-human-factorshci.

technology', since, based on her observation at the time, which probably still holds some truth to date, efforts to study and understand how translation technology assists or hinders translators' work largely come from academia and not developers. But, on the other hand, the human factor is also considered to be a broader component of HCI, less concerned with ergonomics but more to do with understanding how humans interact with computer technology in general and drawing attention to how computer technology plays a role in human lives. This perspective is what I subscribe to in this Element. As mentioned in the previous paragraph, I am interested in understanding how and why translators use the Web and web-based resources and potentially what all this means to translators and their daily practice. Interestingly, roughly around the time when O'Brien introduces the abovementioned concepts of 'human factors' and 'cognitive ergonomics', there is a surge of research in translation studies into 'usability' (a bourgeoning field in HCI) in CAT tools, machine translation, post-editing, and so on (see O'Brien 2010; Cadwell et al. 2016; Doherty and O'Brien 2014).

'Usability' is defined by Preece and colleagues (1994: 722) as 'a measure of the ease with which a system can be learned or used, its safety, effectiveness and efficiency, and the attitude of its users towards it'. The main goal of usability studies is to ensure that users can interact with a UI in quick, easy, successful and gratifying ways (Nielsen et al. 2005). Worth noting here is that while Doherty and O'Brien (2014) prefer to cite ISO/TR16982's definition of usability as a trinity of components, that is, efficiency, effectiveness and satisfaction, which is largely in line with Preece and colleagues' definitions, contemporary usability studies tend to distinguish a few terms related to usability, such as User Experience and Usability Testing. In contrast to Usability, User Experience is considered to be a broader concept as it is not just concerned with a UI's efficiency, effectiveness and satisfaction but places its emphasis heavily on users' emotional response and perception (da Costa et al. 2019: 30–1). In other words, usability can be considered to be one of the components of the wider User Experience or UX. As for Usability Testing (UT), it often refers to commercial rather than academic studies of usability where there is a burgeoning industry specialising in testing the usability of all manners of commercial UI, such as software, websites, smartphones, apps, gaming, sat nav, flight simulators, and so on. UX's emphasis on users' emotional response and perception is known to be linked to UT, given that UX is at the heart of commercial interests for a UI. These days, UT is not just conducted after a (commercial) product is developed or deployed, but often as a part and parcel of UI product design and development. In other words, both summative and formative UT form an integral part of modern UI design. Retrospective think aloud (RTA) is a common eye tracking-based data collection method in both UX and UT. In the following, I will explain what RTA is and how it differs from a think-aloud protocol.

3.3 Retrospective Think Aloud

Many scholars in Translation Process Research (TPR) who adopt think-aloud protocol (TAP) as a data collection method may initially find the term retrospective think aloud (RTA) problematic. This is because in the development of verbal report methods in cognitive psychology where TAP originates, TAP is also known as concurrent verbal report, which is in direct contrast to retrospective and introspective verbal reports. The main difference between retrospective, introspective and concurrent verbal reports lies in the timing of conducting the verbal reports. A retrospective verbal report is conducted after a task is finished in its entirety, an introspective verbal report is conducted at intervals during a task, but a concurrent verbal report is conducted simultaneously while subjects are doing a task. In the 1990s, TAP was considered to be an updated version of the verbal report method with the advantage of minimising common pitfalls in retrospective and introspective verbal reports where it might be difficult for subjects to remember and report on certain details of the process after a task ends entirely or at intervals during the task. Such difficulties are also linked to issues of subjects' potential self-analysis as opposed to a more objective account of the process during a task. While controversies may exist around TAP itself as a research method both in TPR and in cognitive psychology, the consensus of early TAP adopters in translation studies seems to be that TAP remains a valuable and worthy data collection method, provided it is used in carefully controlled circumstances.

As mentioned in the previous paragraph, in connection with the historical background of TAP as a data collection method in translation studies, RTA appears to be a contradictory concept since it combines the seemingly improbable use of synchronous (i.e. concurrent verbal reports) and asynchronous (i.e. retrospective verbal reports) methods at the same time. This was indeed unthinkable prior to new digital research instruments being developed. Nevertheless, as translation studies (and indeed TPR) began to embrace new digital research instruments, such as keylogging and eye trackers, it became possible to 'have your cake and eat it'. As mentioned in Section 3.1, this is owing to the function of 'gaze replay' in eye-tracking software, which enables translators to re-live their (real-time) translation process synchronously while verbalising their thoughts asynchronously. In other words, this approach commonly used in usability studies has the following dual advantages. It utilises the advantage of using eye trackers by tracking where and when translators' eyes fixate and for how long. Meanwhile, it also utilises the advantage of TAP by eliciting the reasons why translators' eyes fixate on certain passages of the texts or parts of the search engine. As a result, a more comprehensive and richer picture of when, how, where and why translators do what they do can be re-enacted and documented in fine-grained details.

Hansen (1991) at the University of Aarhus, Denmark, is probably one of the first scholars to adopt RTA in the field of usability studies. In his study, the use of a traditional video recording is compared with the use of 'eye mark recording', as a cue to support retrospective verbal reports in software testing. Hansen (1991: 48) finds a significant increase (approximately 50 per cent) in problem-oriented verbal comments in the latter method in contrast to the former one. This is an early indication of RTA's effectiveness as a data collection method. In the last twenty years, there have been many studies offering empirical evidence in support of the plausibility of RTA as a valid research method, not just in usability studies but in many other fields. For instance, Cho et al. (2019) use an eye tracking-based RTA to evaluate the usability of a (mobile phone) health app and conclude that it is highly effective in identifying critical usability issues in the field of medical informatics. In the field of marketing, Tanner and colleagues (2020) investigate consumers' engagement in food packaging using eye tracking-based RTA. They also conclude that the use of RTA data shows many promising results in capturing motivational factors that eye tracking alone simply cannot offer. Additionally, Tanner and colleagues (2020) also comment that the use of RTA may be useful to supplement conscious or semi-conscious (visual) attention captured in eye tracking.

The extensive adoption of eye tracking-based RTA both in and beyond usability studies explains why it is known under many different names, such as cued or (cued-based) retrospective reports, eye movements supported verbal retrospection, (eye tracking) stimulated retrospective think aloud, post-experience eye-tracked protocols, and so on (Holmqvist et al. 2011: 104). It is worth pointing out that among studies adopting RTA as a research method, there are also variations in how eye-tracking cues are used in RTA. In fact, Olsen and colleagues' (2010) study is designed to investigate four different methods of combining eye tracking and RTA data in usability testing: no-cued RTA, video-cued RTA, gaze-plot-cued RTA and gaze-video-cued RTA. Strictly speaking, it can be argued that the first two types of methods are not eye tracking-based RTA at all, given that no-cued RTA is simply a type of retrospection and video-cued RTA is simply a screen-recording or video-prompted retrospective report. What is more relevant for the purpose of the present Element is the comparison of the latter two types of RTA, gaze-plot-cued RTA and gaze-video-cued RTA. In eye tracking software, a gaze plot is basically a 2D or static image of subjects' cumulative visual attention, including fixation and tracks of eye movements. A fixation is normally represented in blue dots. The bigger the dots the longer the fixation. Eye movements are normally shown with blue lines. In contrast, gaze replay or gaze video is a live recording with real-time eye movements superimposed on the screen. Unsurprisingly, the results demonstrate that no-cued RTA produces the least amount of data while gaze-video-cued RTA produces the greatest amount of data both in terms of its quantity and variety. This is part of the reason why gaze-video-cued RTA is adopted in this Element.

As mentioned in the previous paragraph, RTA is known under many different names. One of them is post-experience eye-tracked protocols (PEEP). As early adopters of this method in usability studies, Ball and colleagues (2006: 15) describe five stages or steps to conduct PEEP.

Stage 1: A user's eye movements are recorded using a non-intrusive eye tracker while they undertake an interaction task.

Stage 2: The eye-movement trace is replayed to the user in real time as an overlay on the dynamic record of screen-based activity, so as to provide visual cues as to where they were looking during task performance.

Stage 3: The user is requested to use the dynamic replay of their eye-movement trace as a cue to encourage retrospective reporting of task-based activity.

Stage 4: The resulting retrospective verbal protocols are coded and analysed by trained evaluators to determine usability issues associated with the interface.

Stage 5: Recommendations for interface redesign and improvement are established and are referred back to clients.

Apart from RTA, it is important to clarify that it is possible to combine eye tracking and think aloud at the same time. This is known as (eye tracking-based) concurrent think aloud (or CTA) in usability studies. This means that a subject is asked to think aloud and conduct a given task at the same time as an eye tracker is tracking the subject's eye movements in the background. CTA is also used in eye tracking studies in adjacent disciplines outside translation studies. Many of them even compare and contrast the use of CTA versus RTA as data collection methods (see Bowers and Snyder 1990; Gero and Tang 2001; Van Den Haak et al. 2003). The general consensus, however, is that collecting eye tracking data and think aloud data at the same time (i.e. CTA) is only recommended under very specific conditions, the reason being that think aloud is believed to 'mess up' eye tracking metrics due to the extra cognitive load it may impose. An accurate measurement of fixation durations (linked to cognitive load) is of paramount importance in eye tracking research. The only exception is in certain circumstances where a research question is related to the extra cognitive load imposed by certain visual stimuli (Holmqvist et al. 2011: 103). For instance, in educational psychology, CTA is found to be useful in studying how certain reading materials or screen setup (i.e. visual stimuli) may affect a learner's cognitive workload, which may hinder learning as a result.

3.4 Data Collection Procedures

In the study this Element focuses on, a group of twenty-one student and professional translators (students n=11, professionals n=10) were recruited to translate a medical text from English into their mother tongues. The ST (136 words) was abstracted from a medical case report, titled 'Paraplegia follows epidural' from the following website: www.medicalprotection.org/hongkong/casebook-resources/case-reports/case-reports/paraplegia-follows-epidural.

The translators' language combinations included (in alphabetical order) English–Arabic, English–Chinese, English–German, English–Japanese, English–Russian and English–Spanish. All participants were recruited either via an open call or the snowballing method. Their participation was voluntary. The professional cohort had a wide range of professional backgrounds, including legal translation, medical translation, audio-visual translation, literary translation and localisation. The student cohort was recruited from the postgraduate translation programmes (both MA and MSc) at my home academic institution, University College London, UK. Ethical approval was obtained and all necessary procedures were followed. A gift voucher was offered after each participant took part in the study.

The ST was presented in a Microsoft Word document, font size 18. The default web browser was Google Chrome zoomed at 150 per cent for ease of tracking visual attention. Participants were given simple instructions to translate the ST into their mother tongue and to use the Web whenever or wherever they deemed necessary. No time limit or any other restrictions were imposed. Immediately after translating, participants were cued to think aloud retrospectively while viewing the real-time gaze replay recording.

The data collection took place in an office with ample natural light at my home academic institution. The eye tracker used was a SMI 250 Mobile (with a sample rate of 250 Hz). Standard six-point calibration was conducted using SMI iView software prior to the data collection. Calibration procedures were repeated if necessary. SMI's BeGaze software was used to play the gaze replay and record the RTA simultaneously.

4 Findings and Discussion

This section will seek to answer the questions posed in Table 1 (see Section 1), largely following the order of the three themes stated: the use of online resources

(Section 4.1), query-related behaviour in search engines (Section 4.2) and clicking and browsing-related behaviour in search engines (Section 4.3). Relevant
information theories (as reviewed in Section 2) will be drawn on to frame
discussion and support the empirical findings throughout this section.

4.1 The Use of Web-Based Resources

This subsection will not just focus on what web-based resources are used, but
perhaps more importantly on how and why translators use online resources the
way they do. This is because the types of web-based resources used have been
well documented in previous studies, as shown in Section 2. For instance, Massey
and Ehrensberger-Dow (2011a) report that student translators tend to use online
dictionaries whereas instructors tend to use parallel texts and search engines.
Gough (2016: 131–73) also reports an extensive list of online resources and how
frequently they are used by professional translators. Search engines are the top of
the list as the most frequently used online resource. This is followed by bilingual
dictionaries and online encyclopaedia (i.e. Wikipedia). Discussion forums, corpora, online glossaries and Google Translate (NMT: Neural Machine Translation)
also feature in her list. Similar varieties of online resources are also found by Shih
(2017: 53–4) and Cui and Zheng (2021b: 62–3) to be used by their postgraduate
Chinese student translators. The fact that search engines are commonly found to
be one of the most used online resources warrants some attention, not least
because unlike the use of bilingual dictionaries, few details are known about
this process. Therefore, the use of search engines will form a substantial part of
the discussion in this Element. To sum up, previous studies have consistently
shown that (bilingual) dictionaries and search engines are the two most frequently
used online resources by translators, even though some variations in terms of
translators' levels of experience and language combinations inevitably play a role
in their preference and idiosyncratic behaviour when using them. In the following, I will elaborate on further features of translators' use of online resources
based on the empirical data elicited.

4.1.1 General and Idiosyncratic Use of Web-Based Resources

In terms of the use of search engines, this Element shows that some translators
prefer to stick to Google exclusively, while others prefer to use a more varied
combination of web-based resources, such as Google, Baidu (a Chinese search
engine), bilingual corpora (e.g. Linguee) and several different types of online
dictionaries (e.g. monolingual, bilingual, specialised dictionaries and thesauruses).
In other words, in common with previous studies, this Element also confirms that
most translators as a whole use overlapping types of web-based resources, although

individual translators, be they trainees or professionals, have their own idiosyncratic preferences. Several factors are found to be at play here. Language combination is one of them. For instance, most translators invariably use Google as their sole search engine. This is probably owing to the fact that Google is not only one of the most popular search engines around the world, but also the search engine that supports multiple languages. In this Element, Arabic, Japanese, French, German, Russian and Spanish translators all rely on Google as their sole search engine. In fact, Google is often their first port of call for any information seeking on the Web. However, interestingly, such phenomena do not apply to Chinese translators. Instead, Baidu alongside Google are their choices of search engine. This is partly because Google was pulled out of the Mainland Chinese market in 2010 due to censorship rows with the Chinese authorities. As a result, Google has not been available in China since then. It has to be clarified though that this does not mean that Google no longer supports Chinese as a language. As a matter of fact, Google remains the most popular search engine in Hong Kong, Taiwan, Singapore and other Chinese-speaking regions and communities around the world.[4] Given that the data collection was conducted in the UK for the present Element, the Chinese translators had access to both Google and Baidu. On the one hand, some deliberately forego Google and prefer Baidu, citing the reason that Baidu represents a more reliable and comprehensive source of information in Simplified Chinese. On the other hand, there are also individual Chinese translators choosing to use Google predominately rather than Baidu, citing the reason that it has gradually become a habit to use Google. For instance, Subject P20, a student translator, states in her RTA: 'Recently, I am finding myself relying on Google a lot more, probably because I am writing my dissertation at the moment and consult Google more.' Subject P20 reflects that she is largely using Google rather than Baidu as her search engine of choice. This change of preference is probably due to her recent practice of adopting Google for her dissertation writing in English. This demonstrates how a translator can gradually form a collection of web-based resources via their daily use of the Web, and probably not from their translation experience exclusively. Such usages can easily be influenced by other external factors, be they academic, geographical, cultural or even political. To a certain extent, this reveals the reality of translators' work; that is, they cannot be 'immune' to the wider digital landscape that they have little control of. The use of search engines very much typifies these ever-changing influences and dynamics, particularly because search engines are not just used exclusively for translation purposes, but also for other information purposes in translators' daily lives.

---

[4] See www.statista.com/statistics/1128881/taiwan-market-share-of-search-engine-websites/.

As mentioned in the previous paragraph, search engines are among the most used web-based resources by translators. A question that arises here though is whether search engines should be considered a type of web-based resource at all, given that search engines represent a gateway to other information resources on the Web, rather than an information source per se. The empirical data in this Element reveals that search engines alone are indeed used by many translators as an independent source of information, rather than just a gateway to other information on the Web. In other words, it is not just a means to an end, but also an end in itself. For example, Shih (2021: 86) reports that one of her subjects is rarely found to click on any hyperlinks in SERPs. She suggests that there are no real incentives to click on any hyperlinks, given that snippets provide sufficient information to satisfy a subject's query intent. This subject is not the only translator who does this though. In fact, it is shown in this Element that not clicking on any hyperlinks is very much a routine behaviour shared by many translators, rather than an exception. It can be said that translators are effectively using the search engine as if it were a dictionary. Snippets in SERPs represent dictionary entries, albeit at a much larger scale. Translators' decisions to click or not to click in SERPs is determined by a variety of different factors, not just by their query intent alone.

One possible reason for translators' non-clicking behaviour is probably because web search largely represents approximately a third of the whole translation process (see Cui and Zheng 2021a, 2021b; Gough 2016) and often occurs early in the process (see Hvelplund 2019). In other words, for most translators, web search is only an initial vehicle or a problem-solving tool for them to start or to continue to translate. It is an initial and necessary 'hoop to jump through' so to speak, so that they can get on with their real task, which is to translate. In addition, translators are often faced with a large list of queries triggered by the ST, particularly when the ST consists of specialised terminology or content. This is coupled with the fact that translators are likely to be acutely aware of the amount of time it could take to go through each of these queries. From this perspective, keeping an eye on the amount of time and effort spent on web search and making sure that no more time than necessary is invested is very much a necessity. Therefore, it is perhaps no surprise that translators are inclined to save time by not clicking on hyperlinks at all in SERP. This is in spite of the fact that in the study reported in this Element and in many previous studies, no time limit was imposed on translators. In fact, time-saving comments can be repeatedly found in the RTA data in this Element, such as, 'instead of waiting for a webpage to load, I go back to read other snippets'; 'at this point, I decide to just translate it roughly rather than spending more time searching. Will come back later for this problem'; 'copy and paste will save me time from typing this word', and so on.

The other possible reason for not venturing out of search engines is probably related to the 'satisficing strategy' (see Section 2.1). As mentioned in Section 2.1, according to Pirolli's Information Foraging Theory (2007), an information user does not always exhaust all the information available but focuses on locating 'good enough' information before ending their search. From translators' point of view, if the SERP itself provides sufficient information to solve their translation problems, it is naturally unnecessary to click on any hyperlinks at all. A third reason is likely to be the effect of the 'Google generation' (i.e. shallow reading, power browsing and constant flickering between different web-based information), as pointed out by Gough (2016: 33). In other words, translators' use of search engines may be a manifestation of the way humans process digital information on the Web where short bursts of information processing are much preferred over lengthy and laborious ones. Snippets being short bursts of information in the SERP therefore represent more favoured information sources than those presented in external webpages outside search engines.

4.1.2 Ad-hoc and Evolving Use of Web-Based Resources

In Section 4.1.1, the dynamics of how translators may gradually form and change their accustomed habits of collection of web-based resources were partially presented. Adding on to this, further empirical evidence will be presented in this section to show how this formation process may take place on an ad-hoc basis. The following two web search episodes capture this phenomenon.

As Table 2 shows, Subject P18, a student translator, started with the query 'medical dictionary English to Chinese' in Google. She scrolled down the SERP and then selected one of the hyperlinks, which is Dr Dict (an online medical dictionary). At first, she used Dr Dict frequently and commented that she was trying to get used to this new online dictionary. Her (eye-tracked) visual attention largely confirmed this, as she was scanning around various parts of this online dictionary. Then, when posing the query, 'revision surgery 中文' (Back translation: revision surgery Chinese) in Google, she came across another specialised dictionary, Scidict. She expressed her preference for Scidict over Dr Dict, saying '[Scidict] is a better one with lots of sample sentences'. She also admitted that she did not normally do medical translation. Throughout her entire web search process, she was found to largely rely on these two dictionaries in addition to Google despite her brief encounters with the Cambridge dictionary and Google Translate. To sum up, the web search process of Subject P18 has shown, first of all, that the repeated use of web-based resources can be developed on an ad-hoc basis. It shows the

Table 2 Abstract of Subject P18's web search process.

Queries	Resources used	Retrospective think aloud (RTA)
Medical dictionary English to Chinese	Google	–
coronary	Dr Dict	–
coronary bypass graft	Dr Dict	–
artery	Dr Dict	I am trying to get familiar with this dictionary.
graft	Dr Dict	–
revision	Dr Dict	–
revision surgery	Dr Dict	–
revision surgery	Google	–
revision surgery 中文	Google	–
	Scidict	This is a better one with lots of sample sentences. I don't normally do medical translation.
block	Scidict	–
grafts block	Scidict	–
graft block	Google	–
grafts block 中文	Google	–
consultant anaesthetist	Google	–
consultant 中文	Google	–
会诊医师	Google	–
	Cambridge dictionary	Switch to Cambridge dictionary Still waiting for loading!
thoracic epidural	Scidict	–
thoracic epidural	Dr Dict	–
thoracic	Dr Dict	–
epidural	Dr Dict	–
epidural	Scidict	–
	Google Translate (switch back to a previous SERP)	–
术后镇痛	Google	–
weaning	Scidict	–
术后镇痛	Google	–
提供术后镇痛	Google	–

Table 2 (cont.)

Queries	Resources used	Retrospective think aloud (RTA)
实施麻醉	Google	–
haematoma	Scidict	–
cord	Scidict	–
血肿清除术	Google	–

dynamics that search engines cannot only be used to locate web-based resources that are already known to translators, but there is also a shift to locating new ones for specific translation tasks, particularly when a translator is unfamiliar with a ST domain. As mentioned previously, the use of web-based resources is an ongoing, dynamic and multi-layered process. In this case, it is also a learning process. While using these two ad-hoc online dictionaries, Subject P18 was also learning how to use them better and to evaluate which one was better suited for the translation task at hand or even possibly for a future translation task in a similar domain.

The fact that Subject P18 was a student translator might explain her ad-hoc learning and usage of web-based resources, but it is worth noting that the same could also apply to professional translators. To take Subject P09 (a professional translator) as an example, she also began her web search by using Google. Initially all her queries in Google consistently included a ST term, a comma, 中文 (Back translation: Chinese), a comma and 医学 (Back translation: medicine). For instance, her query for the ST term 'weaning' looked like this: 'weaning, 中文, 医学' (Back translation: weaning, Chinese, Medicine). She reported in her RTA that this query pattern had worked very well for her before. It therefore became something she used on a regular basis in Google. Nevertheless, she subsequently realised that while using this query pattern, her SERP consistently presented her with a hyperlink from one specific online dictionary, Scidict. As a result, in the second half of her web search process, she decided to go to Scidict.com directly for all her subsequent terminology-based queries. Just like Subject P18, Subject P09 also indicated that Scidict was not an online dictionary she had come across previously, but she learned that it seemed to be a useful online dictionary for this translation task. In other words, Subject P09, a professional translator, also learned and evaluated which (ad-hoc) web-based resources were more helpful during the course of her web search process and then adapted her web search behaviour accordingly.

4.1.3 The Use of Machine Translation/Neural Machine Translation

The reason that the use of Machine Translation (MT) and Neural Machine Translation (NMT) is discussed here is because it is considered to be a feature and an integral part of translators' web search process, as reported by previous studies (see Gough 2016; Shih 2017, 2019, 2021). For instance, Gough (2016: 163) finds that approximately 75 per cent of professional translators identify themselves as non-MT users in her large-scale survey. That leaves roughly 25 per cent of professional translators as MT users. Following van Der Meer and Ruopp's findings (2015), Gough (2016) divides these MT users into two groups: search and discovery users, and post-editors. The former represents translators using MT as a web-based resource to find more information, and the latter represents translators using MT for post-editing purposes. She concludes that, overall, the former is increasingly more common and further research is required to investigate how translators use MT as an information resource. This Element can be seen to respond to this call.

Before going any further into the discussion, it is worth clarifying here that translators' use of MT/NMT will only be discussed within the aim of this Element, given that a wider discussion about MT/NMT is beyond its scope. Not too dissimilar to Gough's finding (as mentioned in this subsection, roughly a quarter of translators), empirical data in this Element also show that eight out of twenty-one translators (just over a third) have actively used NMT, such as Google Translate and Baidu Fanyi (i.e. the NMT associated with Baidu, the most popular Chinese search engine) during their web search process. Here, actively using NMT is defined as translators actively posting ST segments into NMT for a TL equivalent. However, the use of NMT is a lot more prevalent when taking into account passive usage of NMT. This is because Google Translate and Baidu Fanyi are both associated with their respective search engines. Modern search engines are AI supported and often offer suggested search results, including NMT results, in the SERP. The consequence of this is that even though translators are not actively pursuing NMT, it still plays a considerable role in translators' web search process. The following example captures this.

As seen in Figure 1, Subject P13 was using Baidu to query the ST term 'wean'. The featured result (shown as the first hyperlink at the top of the SERP) was a result from the NMT Baidu Fanyi (fanyi.baidu.com). This naturally grabbed Subject P13's visual attention. She then subsequently clicked on this featured hyperlink to investigate further.

Part of the reason that Baidu Fanyi (NMT) is presented as the featured link in a prominent position in the SERP is likely because Baidu is essentially

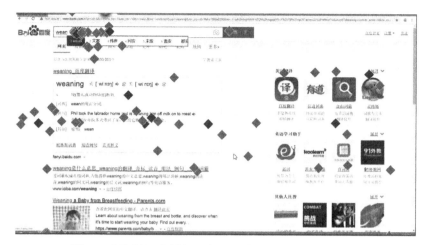

Figure 1 Subject P13's web search for 'wean' in Baidu.

a Chinese search engine that caters for Chinese demographics. This search engine therefore considers Chinese queries as a norm in its search box. When Subject P13 posed an English term 'wean' in its search box, its algorithm assumed that the searcher was looking for a Chinese translation or Chinese definition for this English word. Therefore, the link fanyi.baidu.com (Baidu's NMT) was featured at the top of the page. In fact, the other link, www .iciba.com, one of the popular online dictionaries in China, was also ranked highly in the same SERP, right after the featured NMT result. In other words, the ranker, as mentioned in Section 2.2.1, clearly plays a role here in prompting and pushing dictionaries or dictionary-like results to the top of the SERP. This consequently has an effect on how often Baidu Fanyi (or indeed other NMTs) is used by Chinese translators.

Apart from NMT in search engines, it is also found that NMT is frequently embedded in some online dictionaries. Lingoes, a multilingual online dictionary package, is one example, as indicated in Shih's (2017) study where NMT is routinely presented as one type of (dictionary) entry in Lingoes. In this Element, it is also found that ICIBA and Youdao represent the other two common use of NMT for Chinese translators. ICIBA and Youdao are two online dictionary packages that were originally developed as digitalised versions of multiple paper-based (English–Chinese) dictionaries. However, in recent years, they have been expanded not only to function as online dictionaries but also as NMTs. Just like NMTs associated with search engines, these NMTs can be used independently, but more often than not they are simply embedded in ICIBA and Youdao as dictionary entries. Figure 2 shows an example of Subject P12's use of Youdao and its associated NMT.

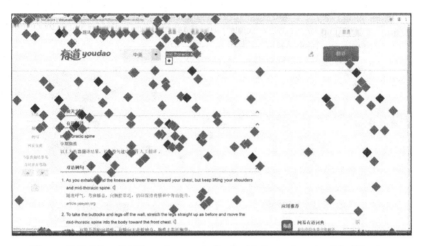

Figure 2 Subject P12's web search for 'mid thoracic spine' in Youdao.

In Figure 2, Subject P12 used the Youdao online dictionary to search for the ST term 'mid thoracic spine' (highlighted in blue). This term could not be found in any of the digitalised paper-based dictionaries in Youdao. However, an NMT solution was shown at the top as an entry, that is, '中期胸椎' (Back translation: middle position thoracic spine). Subject P12 reported in her RTA that 'Youdao offers a NMT solution here. I can see that the sample sentence following the NMT is not quite right either. I don't normally trust NMT solutions. I trust glossaries more'. She then moved on to use the same query in Baidu in her attempt to find out more about this ST term. Interestingly, when Subject P12 posed the same query in Baidu, Baidu Fanyi (Baidu's NMT) was also featured in its SERP prominently. While Subject P12 expressed her reluctance to trust NMT solutions, many other translators in this Element simply accepted NMT results, particularly those embedded in online dictionaries, as if they were trusted dictionary entries.

To summarise, many multi-functional online dictionaries serve as a 'one-stop shop' for translators to solve their translation problems. In fact, this is largely what Shih (2017) finds in her study of student translators. Desktop or app versions of these online dictionary packages can also be downloaded and installed easily. As a result, translators have even easier and sometimes semi-automatic access to them. For instance, ICIBA's desktop version enables translators to simply place a cursor on a ST term for it to activate searches of its multiple online dictionaries and NMTs. It will be interesting for future researchers to focus on how these semi-automatic functions of online dictionary packages may potentially affect translators' web-based information behaviour and translation process with or without the use of CAT tools. Finally, it is important to emphasise that the (passive) use of

NMT for non-postediting purposes is increasingly common and frankly impossible to avoid by translators, given the ways NMT solutions are embedded in modern search engines and online dictionary packages.

4.1.4 The Use of Baidu as a Bilingual Dictionary

In terms of the salient characteristics of how web-based resources are used, this Element also illustrates an interesting phenomenon related to Chinese translators' use of Baidu that is worth closer investigation. Two scenarios are shown in Figure 3 and Figure 4.

Both Figure 3 and Figure 4 show Subject P13's query for the ST term 'coronary artery bypass graft'. In Figure 3, this query was posed in Google and in Figure 4 the same query was posed in Baidu. Obviously, it is important to point out that SERP are tailored to individual searchers; this is because modern search engines are AI supported and designed to learn to customise their SERP depending on each searcher's search history, timing, geographical location, and so on. On the surface at least, it may not always be useful to compare and contrast the use of the same query in different search engines, given that search engines each have their own algorithms. However, it is interesting to illustrate how the translator has deliberately chosen to use these two different search engines in quick succession for the same search query. As mentioned in Section 4.1.1, Baidu is a Chinese search engine. Unlike its counterpart, Google, Baidu's algorithm is designed to predominately cater for the Chinese demographic. When an English term is posed inside the search box of Baidu, its algorithm clearly recognises that this is a non-Chinese query. As a result, Baidu prioritises hyperlinks that offer Chinese definitions for the English

Figure 3 Subject P13's web search for 'coronary artery bypass graft' in Google.

Figure 4 Subject P13's web search for 'coronary artery bypass graft' in Baidu.

query/term in its SERP. As shown in Figure 4, the first hyperlink in Baidu's SERP was a Wikipedia page with a first line of snippet stating '查看此网页的中文翻译, 请点击翻译此页' (Back translation: For Chinese translation of this webpage, please click here). The second hyperlink was from Youdao dictionary. Its snippet offered several Chinese equivalents for the queried ST term. Similarly, the fourth link also offered a Chinese equivalent. This is in direct contrast to Figure 3 where the same ST term was used as a query in Google. Google also identified this query as a term and presented its Knowledge Box on the right-hand side of the SERP. Knowledge Box is a relatively recent addition to Google's algorithm, which automatically recognises certain queries as common terms and presents a short definition (and sometimes pictures) in the SERP. Subject P13, who was translating from English into Chinese, recognised that it was more advantageous for her to use Baidu rather than Google, given that her primary query intent at the time was to locate TL terms. This was why after initially posing her queries in Google, she then decided to dedicate her time to Baidu exclusively throughout her whole web search process. To put it in a different way, she was aware of the different results obtained by inputting ST terms in Google and Baidu, and strategically adapted her web search to use Baidu exclusively as if it were a bilingual dictionary.

4.2 Search Engine Behaviour and Cognition: Query-Related

This subsection will be dedicated to the discussion of translators' use of search engines, particularly related to queries. As mentioned previously in Section 4.1, search engines have been repeatedly identified as among the most frequently used web-based resources in previous studies (see Shih 2017; Cui and Zheng 2021a, 2021b). Queries are important because they represent the first step of a translator's interaction with search engines. As mentioned in Section 2, there are two basic components of HCI: dialogue and interface. Search engines represent the interface that facilitates interaction between human and computer in this instance. When a translator posts a query into a search box, they essentially initiate a dialogue with the computer via this interface. The query represents a 'code' or 'language' used to communicate with search engines. Search engines respond by presenting hyperlinks in the SERP. A translator can then decide how to respond or even whether they want to continue this dialogue. They can choose to respond to this dialogue by clicking on a hyperlink. This then prompts a new dialogue on a webpage outside search engines. At any point of these interactions, a translator can decide to abandon this dialogue (know as query abandonment; see White 2016: 21–37) and/or initiate a new one. Translators' browsing and clicking in the SERP will be discussed in detail in Section 4.3. In this subsection, I will focus on translators' initiation of the dialogue with search engines. It aims to answer the questions of salient characteristics of translators' use of queries in search engines, as seen below.

- What types of queries in search engines do translators tend to use?
- Which query type is more commonly used and why?
- What does query intent entail?
- How and in what circumstances do queries relate to query intent?

4.2.1 Types of Queries and Dominant Query Type

Previous studies (see Shih 2017, 2019, 2021) have identified various types and combinations of queries posed by translators. These include:

- a ST term[/segment];
- a TT term[/segment];
- a ST term[/segment] plus TT equivalent;
- a ST or TT term[/segment] plus Boolean operators or other words to narrow down the search;
- a ST term[/segment] plus a natural language question;
- a natural language question (by itself);
- a ST term[/segment] plus the name of the TL;
- a ST term[/segment] plus its collocating verb;
- a provisionally translated TL term[/segment].

Examples of these query types have been shown and discussed in detail in previous studies (Shih 2017, 2021) and will not be repeated here. Here, I would like to address the 'elephant in the room', a predominant type of query, that is, ST term, in search engines. This is not only found in previous studies but also evident among all the twenty-one translators who took part in the study for this Element.

To understand this query type, it will be useful to first refer to the concept 'Rich Point'. According to PACTE (2011: 41), Rich Point refers to a ST segment that poses a problem and hence triggers problem-solving behaviour in translation. In my previous study (Shih 2019: 7), the concept of Rich Point is used to investigate trainee translators' optimisation of locating TL terms in their web search process. Interestingly, comparable definitions (to Rich Point) can be found in several web search studies with various names, including 'information seeking trigger' (Wang 2018), 'information need' and 'information goal' (Enríquez Raído 2014: 112–46). All these studies have shown that ST terms represent one of the most important initial prompts for web search in translation. What this Element has added to this finding is that ST terms or segments are mostly used directly, intuitively or even conveniently as initial queries in search engines without any alterations whatsoever by translators. In other words, the 'code' translators choose to put forward to search engines is a direct copy-and-paste of ST term(s). Directly copying and pasting ST terms in the search box has the advantage of least cognitive effort at least initially, even though it may have the disadvantage of potentially generating less useful information in the SERP and requiring more cognitive effort subsequently in assessing and sieving through information provided by the SERP. Maximising search results and minimising cognitive effort and time spent on web search have proven to be important considerations for most translators. As mentioned in Section 4.1, translators often adopt the time-efficiency strategy to do so. But it is evident that most translators choose to adopt the approach of investing the least cognitive effort in the first instance for their interactions with search engines. This interesting query behaviour is likely to be a result of several external and internal factors. In terms of the external factors and particularly in a wider digital context, popular search engines, such as Google and Baidu, are keyword-based search engines. Those of us who are old enough to have witnessed the birth of the Internet might remember that first-generation search engines, such as Yahoo and Alta Vista, had an index-based 'facade' that offered a directory of many different websites that a searcher could click on to browse. For a number of years, it was Yahoo rather than Google that dominated the scene of search engines worldwide. But, since its launch in the late 1990s, Google gradually turned the tide to become 'The Search Engine' of the world. Unlike Yahoo,

Google is a true keyword-based search engine that trawls the Web based on queries posed in its search box. After a query is posed, Google presents a series of search results in the SERP. Naturally, translators, as users of Google, are more inclined to use ST terms as their keywords or queries. Apart from this, another possible reason is that to the best of my knowledge, in many of the studies conducted on translators' web search process, including the study presented in this Element, the STs tend to be semi-specialised texts in science, technology and medicine. The nature of these (semi-)LSP texts inherently consists of many ST terms that constitute overt problems for translators to solve. From this point of view, it is no surprise that translators tend to use ST terms as their queries at least initially in their web search process.

4.2.2 Types of Query Intent

Query intent is defined in my previous study (Shih 2021: 76–7) as translators' intention or reasons for posing their queries in search engines. It is important to point out that the concept of query intent differs from similar concepts in previous studies, such as 'information goals' being described as either ST or TT oriented, or 'information needs' as being triggered by ST segments for problem solving (Enríquez Raído 2014: 112–71), in the sense that it focuses on more micro-level and momentary reasons why a particular query is posed in search engines. This is crucial for several reasons. Firstly, query intent has been found to be well suited for depicting the dynamics of translators' web search behaviour, particularly behaviour revealed by the qualitative eye tracking methodology adopted in the study discussed in this Element. Essentially, the concept of query intent acknowledges that an identical query could be linked to multiple query intents. For example, the concept of query intent is particularly useful in analysing why different translators behave very differently on a granulated level when they pose the same query using the same search engine. In addition, query intent should also be distinguished from 'search intent', which is commonly used in IR studies as 'navigational, informational or transactional' (Broder 2002; cf. Shih 2019), given that 'search intent' only offers a generic categorisation of searchers' reasons for either navigating to another website (navigational), finding more information about a topic (informational) or carrying out an action (transactional), none of which provides much analytical value for the present Element.

Query intent is found to play a vital role in translators' decision making in their interaction with search engines. In my previous study (Shih 2021: 84), a list of seven query intents is found among ten professional translators:

1. Locating a TL term.
2. Locating further background information.
3. Validating a TL term or expression.
4. Seeking inspiration for alternative terms or expressions.
5. Locating TL collocation.
6. Post-editing intent.
7. Language-specific intent.

The empirical data reported in this Element largely confirm these query intents. However, they also reveal that there are many other possible query intents in addition to those in this list. In fact, one of the most significant findings about query intent is that it is perhaps not possible to provide an exhaustive list, given that query intents are ever-changing, interacting with the information found in the SERP, preceding queries and also with translators' own background knowledge or personal experiences. In other words, query intent is highly context dependent and unique to each individual translator.

An example of a new query intent can be found in Subject P11's web search for 'cardiac surgery unit', as shown in Figure 5.

Here, Subject P11, a student translator, was seen to pose the query 'cardiac surgery unit'. In her RTA, she reported that at this point, she was trying to check whether 'cardiac surgery unit' was a proper noun or not. In other words, her query intent was neither locating any TL equivalents, nor searching for further background information about the ST term, but solely establishing whether 'cardiac surgery unit' was a proper noun or not; the answer would presumably determine whether she could translate it by herself or if it required her to invest more time and effort in searching for a suitable TL equivalent. According to Subject P11, her confirmation that 'cardiac surgery unit' was indeed a proper noun did not come from any hyperlinks or snippets in the SERP. This was largely reflected in her visual attention captured in the gaze replay where she hardly scrolled down to read the snippets at all; instead, her confirmation came from her noticing a long list of suggested queries (on which her visual attention lingered) in the query box itself. As shown in Figure 5, the query box in Google offered a long list of ten query suggestions, including 'cardiac surgery unit **vgh**', 'cardiac surgery unit **nursing**', 'cardiac surgery unit', and so on. Effectively, this list of suggested queries alone had already fulfilled her query intent and informed her that this ST segment was indeed a proper noun/term. The result of this query intent then led her to form another query intent. Meanwhile, it is worth pointing out that this is yet another prime example demonstrating that translators will always maximise their search

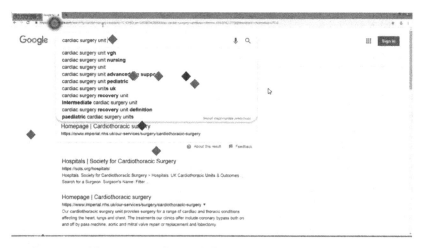

Figure 5 Subject P11's web search for 'cardiac surgery unit' in Google.

results with minimal cognitive effort. It also reveals that translators use search engines creatively. Ultimately, Subject P11's query intent determined her non-clicking and browsing action. From the point of view of HCI, it shows that in search engines, from the very moment when a translator lifts their fingers to type a query, the dialogue with the computer begins. In this example, Google's query suggestions represent a part of the responses from the search engine to the translator. This initial response alone proves to be sufficient to fulfil the translator's intent.

The following example in Table 3 shows the complex dynamics of inter-woven relationships between queries and query intents, as they evolve conse-quentially during the web search process.

In this web search episode (see Table 3), Subject P17 was focusing on the ST term 'consultant anaesthetist'. It took him nine queries associated with multiple query intents to resolve his problem and eventually end this entire web search episode. According to his RTA, initially he was not sure which grade or rank of doctor 'consultant anaesthetist' was. This was his overarching query intent. He started with his first query, 'consultant anaesthetist' in Youdao dictionary. But this query intent was not considered fulfilled because Youdao did not seem to be able to locate any TL equivalent, apart from a Youdao Fanyi (Youdao's NMT) solution. Subject P17 then decided to try another NMT, Google Translate, which returned an identical solution, '顾问麻醉师' (Back translation: consult-ant anaesthetist). He then decided to use this NMT solution as his new query in Baidu. The query intent at this point was to verify whether this NMT solution was a plausible term in the TL, even though he said that he knew it was not. He confirmed that the NMT solution was not a common term in the TL, just as he

Table 3 Abstract of Subject P17's web search process

Queries	Online resources	Retrospective think aloud (RTA)	Query intents	Intent fulfilled?
consultant anaesthetist	Youdao	**I want to know which grade/level of doctor this is.** There is only Youdao MT, 顾问麻醉师, not quite right. I cannot use this.	**- Check which grade or level of doctor this doctor's title is.** **- Locate a TL equivalent.**	No. No.
consultant anaesthetist	Google Translate	I now try to use Google Translate (MT). Google Translate also gives me 顾问麻醉师. I cannot use this.	Same as above	No.
顾问麻醉师	Baidu	**I am trying to double check this TL term exists in Baidu, even though I think it is wrong.** I am right. This does not exist.	**Check whether the NMT solution is a viable one.**	No.
consultant anaesthetist meaning	Google	I know that consultant is a grade or level of UK doctor. But, the trouble is I am not sure there is a equivalent grade in China. I spend some time looking at the suggested queries for clues. Then, I scroll down reading SERP.	- Check which grade/level of doctor this title is.	No.

Query	Search engine	Notes	Strategy	Result
consultant meaning	Google	I am reading the featured dictionary entry in Google, **trying to understand the meaning of 'consultant' in the ST.** It says, 'doctor of senior rank'. I now know that this is a title of a senior doctor.	Same as above.	Yes.
高级麻醉师	Baidu	I try to translate it literally into Chinese and use it as a query in Baidu. See how it goes. **This is not a proper noun.** I click on the 1st hyperlink and read the webpage. **I can see that there is** 主治医师 **and** 主任医师 主任医师 **is a higher ranking than** 主治医师	- Check whether a literal translation exists.	No. But, find some useful info about doctor's ranking in China.
consultant rank in hospital	Google	I know that in English, it is a senior ranking.	- Check whether consultant is the highest ranking.	Yes.

Table 3 (cont.)

Queries	Online resources	Retrospective think aloud (RTA)	Query intents	Intent fulfilled?
		But, **I am not sure whether it is the highest ranking.** **I need to clarify this.** Click on the 1st hyperlink, the BMA link and read this webpage in detail. It says, "the most senior grade in hospitals". Ah, it must be 主任医师		
麻醉主任医师	Baidu	**I am now trying to figure out whether I can put 麻醉 and 主任医师 together in Chinese.** I can see 麻醉主任医师. But, I feel it does not sound right. I can also see 麻醉科主任医师, which sounds better.	- **Check whether 麻醉主任医师 is a viable solution.**	Yes.
麻醉科主任医师	Baidu	I am checking how many results can be found in comparing these two. The latter.	- Bolster the preferred solution, 麻醉科主任医师	Yes.

suspected. Consequently, he decided to try Google again. With two successive queries, 'consultant anaesthetist meaning' and 'consultant meaning' in Google, he was still looking for clues for his original intent, that is, which grade or rank of doctor consultant was. While browsing the SERP in Google, he found that a consultant was referred to as a senior doctor in the featured link at the top of the page. Armed with this new piece of relevant information, he decided to go back to Baidu and pose the query, '高级麻醉师' (Back translation: senior anaesthetist), a literal translation in the TL; the query intent here was to find out whether this literal translation existed in the TL. He concluded that the answer was negative based on his browsing of SERP snippets in Baidu. While browsing the snippets, he decided to click on one of the hyperlinks. This took him to a TL webpage that explained the different ranking of doctors in China. This newly found webpage gave him two relevant titles for doctors, 主治医师 and 主任医师; the latter being a more senior role. This prompted him to go back to Google to find out more about the rankings of British doctors. The query this time was 'consultant rank in hospital'. Again, he chose to click on a hyperlink. This took him to the British Medical Association (BMA) webpage confirming that consultant was the highest rank of doctors in the British medical profession. At this point, he had largely resolved his original goal of finding out what rank or level 'consultant' was and at the same time located the title of a highest-ranking doctor in the TL. According to him, the only issue left (i.e. query intent) was that he was not sure about the collocation of a highest-ranking doctor and anaesthetist in the TL. He cautiously posed a preliminary (literal) translation, '麻醉主任医师' (Back translation: anaesthetic senior doctor) in Baidu, as his query to check whether this was a viable collocation in the TL. Snippets in the SERP showed that this was a probable collocation but there was also an alternative one, which he seemed to prefer. This was when he posed his final query, '麻醉科主任医师' (Back translation: senior doctor of the anaesthetic department) with a query intent to find more evidence to bolster his preference. As his preferred solution could be found in several snippets in the SERP, he decided to conclude this web search episode and adopted it as his translation for the ST term. One interesting feature worth pointing out here is that query intent can have very different properties. Some query intents are purely explorative and open-ended in nature and aim to find out what information is available out there, while other query intents are more fixed and rigid, for example merely for validating or verification purposes. With these more fixed and rigid query intents, as shown in Subject P17's web search episode, translators may have already made up their mind or at least have a strong inkling of what they will find in the SERP. In this case, the underlying objective is to help validate their suspicion or even bolster a pre-determined translation solution. This narrows down their web search to a more targeted way of locating evidence to support their inkling.

To sum up, the web search episode shown in Table 3 has illustrated how an overarching search intent can evolve organically into several micro query intents. This very much epitomises Bates' berrypicking theory (Bates 1989: 410), as shown in Section 2.1. In other words, each query intent is dynamic in the sense that they can be created ad hoc and informed by the finding of a previous query. Each query then provides some more clues and directions for subsequent queries and query intents. Each of the micro query intents gradually brings the translator incrementally closer to their final destination where the overarching search intent is finally fulfilled.

4.3 Search Engine Behaviour and Cognition: Browsing and Clicking

This subsection is dedicated to clicking and browsing behaviours in search engines. As mentioned in Section 3.2, in HCI, while queries represent the initial dialogue of the interaction between translators and computers (via search engines), clicking and browsing behaviour represents the subsequent dialogue. This subsequent dialogue is probably one of the most complex aspects of the web search process, as it epitomises whether an existing dialogue will continue or end, or a brand-new dialogue is initiated, sometimes outside search engines. This subsection focuses on the following.

- Sequences or patterns of browsing and clicking behaviour in translators' interaction in the SERP;
- Reasons and implication of translators' decision not to click on any hyperlinks in the SERP;
- Determining factors involved in translators' clicking and browsing behaviour.

4.3.1 Sequences and Patterns of Browsing and Clicking Behaviour in the SERP

In my previous study (Shih 2021), a diagram of the sequence of translators' clicking and browsing behaviour in search engines is mapped out (see Figure 6). It shows a general pattern or sequence of translators' visual attention (i.e. scanning or reading action) and their active dialogue (i.e. clicking action) with search engines after a query is posed. Typically, translators start with scanning action in the SERP, characterised by their rapid and vertical visual attention. This is when their first judgement of relevance takes place, which determines whether any snippets in hyperlinks are worth reading or not. If not, the sequence will end and move back to a new query. If yes, translators

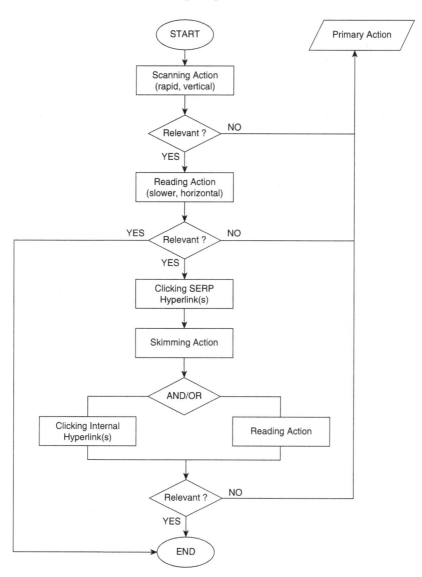

Figure 6 The sequence of translators' browsing and clicking behaviour in search engines.

commence their reading action of the SERP, characterised by slower and horizontal visual attention. The second judgement of relevance takes place at this point. If a snippet or hyperlink is judged to be relevant, translators then click on the relevant hyperlink to investigate further. If not, again, the sequence ends and moves back to a new query. When a hyperlink is clicked or when an external webpage is opened, translators can choose to scan and/or read. This is when the third judgement of relevance takes place. If the judgement of relevance is positive, the whole search sequence comes to an end satisfactorily; if it is negative, it could lead back to the second judgement of relevance again where another hyperlink could be judged relevant and clicked, or it could lead back to a new query. To sum up, there are three points of judgement throughout the sequence of clicking and browsing behaviour. Each of these judgements represents a crossroad that determines whether translators should continue to invest their time and effort by clicking or browsing further or not.

4.3.1a To Click or Not to Click, That Is the Question

Here, I would like to focus on one particular feature or pattern of translators' search engine behaviour, which is 'query abandonment' (White 2016: 21–37; cf. Shih 2019). As mentioned in Section 4.2, in IR studies, query abandonment refers to the circumstance where a searcher chooses not to click on any links in the SERP. As the word 'abandonment' literally suggests, this is an indication of negative and unsatisfactory search engine usage, as it is generally considered to be evidence that a searcher is not happy with the search results and therefore chooses not to interact with the SERP (see Khabsa et al. 2016; Wu and Kelly 2014). Nevertheless, this is not the case for translators, as translators' query abandonment often represents a satisfactory end to the whole search episode. This somewhat aligns with 'good abandonment' phenomena in IR research (see Khabsa et al. 2016; Li et al. 2009) where a searcher decides that the information provided in the SERP itself is sufficient, although it remains a thorny issue in IR studies in terms of how a search engine algorithm is able to predict or even distinguish a 'good' abandonment from a bad one.

As found in my previous study (Shih 2021), not clicking any hyperlinks in SERP or 'good abandonment' is very much a default behaviour rather than an exception in translators' web search process. Empirical data presented in the present Element firmly confirm this exact finding. This is true irrespective of translators' length of experience or whether they are professionals or students. In other words, in interacting with search engines, translators frequently choose not to click on any hyperlinks. Referring back to Figure 6, this unique phenomenon is displayed in the long line on the left between the second judgement of relevance to the end of the diagram. In other words, unlike stereotypical search engine episodes widely reported in IR studies, when translators decide not to click on any hyperlinks, especially after they read and invest their time and visual attention in snippets, it is often an indication that they have already found the information they need satisfactorily, or their query intents have already been fulfilled by snippets alone. Table 4 shows a typical example of this in Subject P09's web search episode.

As seen in Table 4, Subject P09 (a professional translator) chose not to click on any hyperlinks in the SERP but spent her time reading snippets in detail for five different queries. She revealed later in her RTA that her query intent was mostly to locate a suitable TL equivalent for the ST terms. This was also the reason why she used a very consistent pattern of queries in Google: 'ST term, 中文, 医学' (Back translation: ST term, Chinese, Medicine). She conceded that using this query pattern normally generated many useful snippets in both English and Chinese in the SERP. Therefore, she was able to take full advantage of these snippets by comparing and contrasting bilingual information and ultimately located a suitable TL equivalent. There was no need to invest her time and effort in clicking on hyperlinks at all. In other words, SERPs were used as if they were dictionary entries.

Table 4 Abstract of Subject P09's web search process.

Queries	Online resources	Retrospective think aloud (RTA)
thoracic epidural, 医学	Google	This is when I first come across Scidict. com in SERP. I think it is good. So, I use it a lot afterwards. **I read the snippets in detail.**
postoperative analgesia, 中文, 医学	Google	**I read the snippets in detail.** Then, go back to the TT.
weaning, 中文, 医学	Google	I have some personal experience of having surgery and anaesthetics. So, it is easier for me to see what the ST means. **I read the snippets in detail.** Fixate on '脱离呼吸机'.
CT scan, 中文, 医学	Google	**I read the snippets in detail.** SERP shows lots of 'CT'. 'CT' is very commonly used in Chinese. Go back to translation. I cannot see much in the snippets. I did not see 脑电图. I know脑电图is what is normally called in Chinese.
thoracic spine, 中文, 医学	Google	**I read the first 3 snippets** [the first one is the Scidict]

This phenomenon shows that translators' behaviour of 'query abandonment' or 'good abandonment' is incongruent with that of stereotypical web searchers. This is because unlike translators, most web searchers probably do not regularly pose bilingual queries, nor do they use search engines as if they were bilingual dictionaries. In other words, this type of bilingual usage of search engines is largely unique to translators. Yet, the trouble is that by not clicking on any hyperlinks repeatedly and persistently after posing queries, the translators may unknowingly put forward a message or dialogue to the computer (via the search engine algorithm) that the search results in the SERP are unsatisfactory. In other words, a form of unintended miscommunication may take place between search engines and translators, partly due to a general assumption that when a searcher poses a query, a natural progression is to click on a hyperlink. It is no wonder that translators can sometimes find it difficult to locate useful information in search engines. In a wider context outside translation studies, this reveals a perennial difficulty of search engine algorithms, which is well beyond the scope of this Element; that is, it is extremely challenging for computer engineers to build a search engine (algorithm) that can cater for every single type of searcher, including translators.

In addition to 'query abandonment', over the years, a great deal of literature has been dedicated to studying typical behaviours of search engine users. The most prominent of these is probably that most searchers typically only browse and click on the first few hyperlinks listed at the top of the SERP (see Granka et al. 2004; Joachims et al. 2007). This is the reason why advertisements and sponsored links are always positioned near the top of the SERP. This also contributes to a series of SERP designs and layout features in commercial search engines. As mentioned in Section 4.1.4, there is a relatively new feature in Google called 'Knowledge Box' or 'knowledge graph' (Ceri et al. 2013). The 'knowledge box' is known to be 'integrated in the search [engine] interface and provides basic information about the search topic' (Ludolph et al. 2016). As the name suggests, 'Knowledge Box' is 'framed' in a box and normally positioned at the top right-hand corner of the SERP side by side with other high-ranking hyperlinks (to the left). Google's 'Knowledge Box' often directly cites topical information about a search query from a popular database, such as Wikipedia, displaying a hyperlink acknowledging the information source at the bottom of the box (Ludolph et al., 2016). 'Knowledge Box' is sometimes accompanied by an image from the data source as well. Different search engines have different design features and layouts in their SERPs. Figure 7 shows an alternative example in Baidu, the popular Chinese search engine.

In this example, the query 'graft' was posed as a query in Baidu. Unlike Google, Baidu displayed a collection of recommended e-resources (in the form of

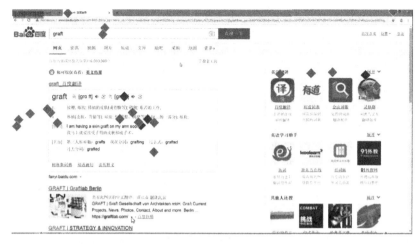

Figure 7 A screenshot of web search for 'graft' in Baidu.

thumbnails) at the top right of the SERP that its algorithm considers to be relevant. In this example, a number of different NMTs, online dictionaries along with a few web-based resources for learning English were displayed as a result.

No doubt all these new SERP features and layouts in either Google or Baidu are designed to draw searchers' visual attention. For translators, while it is possible that their visual attention may well be drawn to these featured and framed results, it is also common for them to skip them altogether. In fact, empirical evidence in this Element suggests that content displayed, especially at the top right of the SERP, such as 'Knowledge Box' or 'thumbnails', is often ignored by translators. The downside of this is that translators may run the risk of missing potentially vital information. The flipside of this, however, is that they can concentrate on looking for and assessing what appears to be the most important information for them at the time. To a certain extent, the fact that translators choose not to be distracted by novel layouts in the SERP probably reflects their experience and knowledge of using search engines. It is also possible that this is merely a reflection of their time-efficiency strategy. As discussed in Section 2, web search typically accounts for up to a third of the entire translation process. From translators' point of view, it is vital for them not to let this process take over the whole translation process. Therefore, having a laser-sharp focus when going through a huge amount of information presented in search engines is a useful and necessary strategy.

4.3.1b Other Typical Clicking and Browsing Behaviour

Another typical clicking and browsing behaviour of translators is a constant and rapid switching between different opened webpages and SERPs both in the pre-drafting phase and during the drafting phase. As mentioned in Section 2.3.2, Cui and Zheng (2021b: 68) identify a very similar phenomenon in their study. According to them, this phenomenon is related to the perceived difficulty of the translation task. In other words, the more difficult trainees perceive the translation task to be, the more they exhibit rapid switching behaviour on the screen due to cognitive overload. Cui and Zheng (2021b: 68) argue that an important pedagogical implication of this finding is that trainee translators should be trained to improve their working memory capacity, presumably to avoid the rapid switching phenomenon. It seems that the switching back and forth between different webpages and SERPs is considered to be a negative feature in web search. While this may be true for student translators in Cui and Zheng's study, evidence in this Element suggests that this is not always the case, as this phenomenon is shared by experienced professional and student translators alike. In fact, the RTA data in this Element (e.g. 'instead of waiting for a webpage to load, I go back to read other snippets') has shown that the rapid switching phenomenon can simply be a reflection of translators' time-efficiency strategy because many translators prefer to fully utilise their time by switching to other webpages or SERPs rather than staying idle waiting for a webpage to be loaded. But, more significantly, this may also be a manifestation of translators' strategy of using opened webpages or SERP as a form of external memory to supplement their overloaded working memory. This is because when translators try to tackle a complex translation problem via web search, inevitably they are bombarded with many sources of information in various forms. It may be very difficult for them to keep hold of every single piece of information while their working memory is hard at work. By switching back and forth rapidly and repeatedly between these information sources, their visual attention (or sensory input) is able to register them temporarily or keep hold of them a little longer in their working memory so as to assist the complex decision-making process. In other words, the behaviour of rapidly going back and forth to different information sources may not be a liability or an expression of anxiety but a strategy for translators to ease their overloaded working memory. Therefore, in my opinion, the pedagogical implication should not be so much about training and improving the capacity of translators' working memory, given that working memory will always have its maximum capacity. Instead, the pedagogical implication should be about acknowledging that there are cognitive and behavioural mechanisms that translators can learn to adopt in order to mitigate overloaded working memory in web search. Indeed, rapidly switching back and forth between different information sources represents one of the useful mitigation strategies for doing so.

4.3.2 What Determines Clicking and Browsing Behaviour

As mentioned in Section 4.3.1, the moment at which translators make their decision regarding their browsing and clicking behaviour depends on the three points of judgement of relevance. Two aspects will be addressed here: the concept of judgement of relevance and what sources of information translators are actually judging.

First of all, I would like to focus on translators' judgement of relevance. In search engine research, 'relevance of judgement' is a term used to refer to the criteria that searchers use to judge how relevant information is in the SERP and external webpages. Also known as 'credibility judgement' (Kattenbeck and Elsweiler 2019), these criteria include ranking, recency, topicality, specificity, scope and (information) quality (see Savolainen and Kari 2006). In other words, searchers are judging information based on their ranking position in the SERP, how recently the information was produced and whether the information presented is of high quality, and so on. Incidentally, this is very similar to what translation textbooks (see Austermühl 2014) sometimes dub part of the 'information literacy' or 'instrumental competence' that translators should possess, given that it is vital for translators to assess the reliability of any information they come across on the Web. While it is no doubt useful to know what the general criteria of judgement of relevance may be, these criteria fall short of illustrating translators' clicking and browsing behaviour in detail. In other words, what distinguishes this Element from many previous studies is that it demonstrates an intricate mechanism of judgement of relevance on a granulated level in the context of translation that is constantly adjusting and altering, pending the ad-hoc context of the preceding or subsequent queries, search results and other clicking (non-clicking) browsing decisions, and so on. Each granulated judgement and decision feeds into a subsequent and ultimately final one. More importantly, these granulated judgement criteria are found to link to query intents directly. In other words, translators' cognition and behaviour in search engines are determined by how relevant they judge or 'interpret' the information to be fulfilling their query intent (as shown in Subject P17's RTA in Table 3; see Section 4.2.2).

There are two factors here: the judgement of relevance and the information that translators are judging. On the surface, the information that translators use to make their judgement of relevance is presumably any content or information presented to them in the SERP after their query is posed or content presented in an external website/webpage once a hyperlink is clicked. In terms of the information in the SERP, it can be presented in many different shapes and forms, such as 'Knowledge Box', NMT solutions and suggested queries.

How and where these different types of content are presented in the SERP have been covered in Section 4.3.1 and will not be repeated here. Instead, further details about the list of hyperlinks and their associated information will be addressed in the following. In most commercial search engines, the list of hyperlinks in the SERP comprises the following information: the title of the hyperlink itself, URL, snippet and occasionally an image. In addition to this, the query (term) is normally highlighted in red in Baidu or in bold in Google. Highlighting is found to be very useful for translators. This is because when translators frequently pose ST terms/segments as queries, these highlighted terms in snippets serve as 'visual spotlights' to guide translators' visual attention and cognition. There is evidence in this Element to suggest that this highlighting feature becomes a design feature that helps shape translators' information behaviour in search engines. This is shown in Figure 8 and partially in Table 4 (Section 4.3.1) where Subject P09 was searching for TL equivalents for the ST term 'CT scan'.

In her RTA, Subject P09 articulated that 'SERP shows lots of "CT". "CT" is commonly used in Chinese … I did not see 脑电图 (Back translation: EEG). I know that 脑电图 is what CT is normally called in Chinese.' Here, Subject P09's query intent was not locating a TL equivalent for the query 'CT scan', but rather to verify what she thought she knew, which was (1) 'CT' does not need to be translated; (2) 'CT scan' stands for 脑电图 in the TL. Therefore, her judging criteria were guided by these query intents, that is, whether she could find enough information in the SERP to support her existing knowledge about 'CT scan'. Obviously, 'CT scan' and 'EEG' are two different types of medical imaging tools, and Subject P09 made the error of mixing the two in her

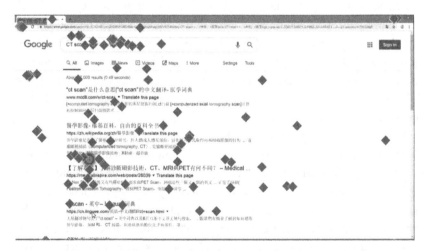

Figure 8 Subject P09's web search for 'CT scan' in Google.

long-term memory. This web search episode demonstrates an interesting example of what happens when the external information sought in the SERP appears to contradict internal information from one's long-term memory. After some weighing up, Subject P09 consequently decided to translate 'CT scan' into 脑电图 based on her long-term memory. This resulted in a translation error.

A fascinating part of this example is that the correct TL equivalent for 'CT scan' was actually shown in the snippet of the second hyperlink, that is '电脑断层扫描 (Back translation: Computerised Tomography Scan)', even though it was not highlighted in red or in blue unlike the term 'CT'. As a result, this piece of vital information was apparently missed by Subject P09 when she visually scanned through the snippets. There are likely to be two reasons for this. Firstly, when she scanned the snippets (rather quickly), her visual attention only focused on the highlighted terms in the snippets. This in itself is likely to be a result of her previous experiences of scanning the highlighted terms being sufficient for her to solve her translation problems. Query Term Highlighting (QTH) in snippets is a common feature in commercial search engines (Zhang 2018). The assumption behind this feature (based on IR research) is that highlighting will serve as a visual aid for searchers to decide which hyperlinks are worth clicking. In other words, highlighting itself is a feature that is designed to make the highlighted segments become more visually salient or 'eye-catching'. Therefore, it is no surprise that translators' visual attention is drawn to them. In most cases, this feature in snippets serves translators well, largely because translators often use SERP listings as dictionary entries and ST terms as queries. Nevertheless, what this example has revealed is that sometimes it can backfire if translators are too drawn to the highlighted words rather than other information in the snippets. The truth is that in pursuing optimisation in web search, it is important to remember that efficiency should never precede effectiveness in translators' web search, as discussed in Shih's (2019) study. This finding also shows a possible reason behind a classic scenario which Massey and Ehrensberger-Dow (2011b) have characterised in their study as the 'looking but not seeing' phenomenon where translators fail to notice or process the most useful information presented to them on the computer screen. The other likely reason for ignoring a correct TL equivalent in snippets in Subject P09's case was that there was a competing TL equivalent in her long-term memory, and at this point her judgement of relevance might be searching for evidence to confirm or support her existing knowledge. This is often known as 'confirmation bias' (Nickerson 1998) in psychology, as most people generally prefer information that supports rather than counts against their existing views or values. In other words, at this point, her real underlying query intent was probably to bolster a TL equivalent she assumed she knew. It is as if her visual attention (as guided by her query intent) automatically 'censored' or 'suppressed' irrelevant information that did not support her existing knowledge. This again demonstrates the complexity and dynamics between query intent and judgement of relevance from external information (including the highlighting feature in the SERP) and internal knowledge.

Dervin's (1983) Sense-Making Theory and Kuhlthau's (1990, 1991) affective factors in information seeking, as mentioned in Section 2.1, can also be used to explain this web search episode, as they denote that human beings make sense of or understand the world by constantly referring back and forth between (new) external information and (existing) internal knowledge. This understanding then becomes a basis for them to act upon. In this example, during Subject P09's web search episode, the judgement of relevance from external information had to compete and interact with internal knowledge. While uncertainty and hesitation could be observed due to incongruence or conflicting information, internal knowledge clearly overrode the external information sought in this instance.

To sum up, the query intent and information encountered in the SERP have a complex and intertwining relationship in translators' cognition and behaviour in using search engines. Referring back to Figure 6 in Section 4.3.1, each of the three points of judgement represents a crossroad or juncture of what to do next. The criteria of this judgement (of relevance) are based on a momentary and sometimes evolving query intent or, in other words, how closely the information comes to fulfilling the query intent at the time. The information being judged though is not just limited to external information presented in the SERP or on webpages, but crucially also include translators' own internal knowledge in their long-term memory.

5 Conclusion

This Element reports an investigation of translators' web search process. It focuses on three themes: translators' use of web-based resources along with two aspects of translators' search engine behaviours, including those related to queries and those related to browsing and clicking.

With regard to the first theme (see Section 4.1), the use of web-based resources, it is found that the most frequently used web-based resources are online dictionaries and search engines, echoing similar findings in many previous studies. Unsurprisingly, Google 'tops the chart' as the most used search engine by most translators. However, unlike translators in other language combinations, Chinese translators tend to use Baidu and Google as their search engines of choice. While translators tend to use similar types of web-based resources, their actual resources used evolve over time and can be used on an ad-hoc basis. In fact, it is found that when using search engines, both student and professional translators do not just constantly assess information found in the SERP, but also assess new and potentially useful web-based resources so that they can be adopted on the fly or potentially in the future. With regard to the use of NMT, just like previous studies, this Element shows that translators regularly use NMT as a web-based resource. However, this Element also reveals that the use of NMT is a lot more prevalent than previous studies may have suggested. This is because NMT outputs are often incorporated as part of the search results in search engines and as dictionary entries in online dictionary packages. As a result, translators are using NMT solutions even without actively seeking to use them. This finding also suggests that most translators probably do not post-edit NMT output but treat it as one piece of independent information among many other pieces of information found on the Web for them to 'pick and mix' from.

With regard to the second theme (see Section 4.2), query-related cognition and behaviour in search engines, query types uncovered in previous studies have also been largely identified in the present Element. What is noteworthy though is that the single most employed query type is a direct adoption of ST terms/segments to the query box. In other words, most translators habitually copy and paste a ST term/segment into the search box as their query. Apart from being a matter of convenience, this is likely due to the fact that modern search engines are keyword-based search engines. In the context of translation, ST terms/segments are effectively keywords for relevant information being sought. The ST terms/segments also represent 'information seeking triggers' that initiate the problem-solving and web search process in translation. Therefore, it is logical to use ST terms/segments as queries directly. While the copy-and-paste query behaviour gains in terms of 'no-fuss' convenience, it may subsequently result in lengthy and laborious processes to decipher relevant information in the SERP. Translators can of course choose to strategically invest more time and effort in planning and formulating sophisticated queries so as to narrow down their search results in the hope that such effort will pay off in the end. It is speculated that perhaps past experiences taught them that (cognitive) investment in refining queries does not always pay off or guarantee success. Therefore, most translators simply copy and paste ST terms/segments directly without much deliberation.

Unlike query types, it is difficult to exhaust a list of query intents. To reiterate, query intent is a term that was first used by Shih (2021: 76–7), which conceptualises moment-to-moment inferences and motivation that lead to a query being posed. The concept of query intent is useful in scrutinising the complex and multi-layered interaction between queries, browsing and clicking behaviour in web search. Part of the reason that it is impossible to exhaust the list of query intents is that query intents are highly context dependent, individualised and ever-evolving according to different contextual factors, such as the outcome of a previous query, incongruence between query results and existing knowledge, and even translators' own past web search experiences. Each of these contextual factors can play a role in contributing to the formation of query intents and consequently dictate web search behaviour.

With regard to the third theme (see Section 4.3), translators' browsing and clicking behaviour, a model of translators' browsing and clicking behaviour has been mapped out (see Figure 6), illustrating sequential patterns of translators' web search process in search engines. In this model, there are three points of judgement. Each point determines whether translators should continue to browse, click, post a new query or abandon the whole web search episode. These judgement points are largely guided by translators' query intent, in particular, how well the elicited information fulfils the relevant query intent. In terms of what translators are judging, it is important to point out that they are not just judging information relevance as presented in the SERP, but also how such information fares against their own internal knowledge and past experiences. After all, this is how translators 'make sense' of information available to them and solve their translation problems accordingly. Occasionally, translation errors can occur as a result of direct conflicts between the elicited information in search engines and the knowledge possessed in translators' long-term memory.

One of the most interesting findings presented in this Element is probably the default behaviour that translators rarely click on hyperlinks in the SERP. A variety of reasons may be at play, including time efficiency and the 'satisficing' strategies adopted by translators. Another reason is likely to be the 'Google generation' effect, as briefly mentioned by Gough (2016). The so-called Google generation (web users) are said to 'skitter over the surface of the web rather than going deep into particular areas'.[5]

While the non-clicking behaviour has not gone unnoticed in search engine research outside translation studies, given this phenomenon is known as 'query abandonment' or 'good abandonment', what is unique in the context of translators' web search is that this seems to be the default behaviour rather than the exception. In the wider context of HCI, this default behaviour potentially results in disjointed communication between translators (i.e. human) and search engines (i.e. computer). After all, search engines are designed to be a gateway to the Web. While it is true that translators do use search engines as stepping stones for external web-based resources, they often, in fact, predominantly use them as

---

[5] See https://blogs.ucl.ac.uk/digital-education/2010/02/21/what-is-the-google-generation/.

a source of information in their own right. It is well beyond the scope of this Element to gauge potential implications of this phenomenon for search engine algorithm and UI design. What this Element has successfully attained though is to contribute to the continuous endeavour in the field of HIB in understanding the highly complex and context-dependent information behaviour of translators.

Within the field of translation studies, this Element has two main contributions to make. The first is that it is one of the first studies to embark on a systematic investigation of translators' use of search engines. It focuses on translators' queries, browsing and clicking behaviour within search engines. Future research directions could 'hone in' on translators' web search behaviour that derives from but occurs outside search engines and how such behaviour may impact translation activities as a whole. Translators working in different contexts, genres, modes and language combinations could also be investigated individually and comparatively. In addition, it will be interesting for future researchers to ascertain in what ways or which parts of translators' web search behaviour are specific or unique to translators rather than other types of web users. The second significant contribution of this Element lies in its qualitative approach to eye tracking research. This Element is unique in the sense that, to the best of my knowledge, it is one of the first pieces of research in translation studies that challenges the status quo and demonstrates that a qualitative eye tracking methodology is not only feasible but also effective in answering research questions that a quantitative eye tracking approach cannot address. I believe that two decades after O'Brien first introduced eye tracking into translation studies, there is room for an alternative and equally valid approach to eye tracking research in our field.

We live in an era of increasing dominance and reliance on the Web and web-based technology. This is no exception for translators. Almost every aspect of translators' work is bound to be framed and affected by the wider digital landscape. There is still so much unknown to be learned and discovered. In many ways, I hope that this Element serves as a beginning, not an end, to a quest of continuous learning and discovery about translators and the Web.

Finally, for readers who are interested in practical suggestions about the use of search engines, I have created a short video titled 'Hints and tips: Translators' use of search engines', www.cambridge.org/Shih_pptx.

References

Aula, A., Majaranta, P. and Räihä, K. J., 2005. Eye-tracking reveals the personal styles for search result evaluation. In M. F. Costabile and F. Paternò (eds.) *Human-Computer Interaction – INTERACT 2005*. Berlin: Springer, pp. 1058–61.

Austermühl, F., 2014. *Electronic Tools for Translators*. New York: Routledge.

Ball, L. J., Eger, N., Stevens, R. and Dodd, J., 2006. Applying the PEEP method in usability testing. *Interfaces*, 67(Summer): 15–19.

Bates, M. J., 1989. The design of browsing and berrypicking techniques for the online search interface. *Online Review*, 13(5): 407–24.

Beutelspacher, L., 2019, July. Dr. Google, please help me understand! In G. Meiselwitz (ed.) *International Conference on Human-Computer Interaction*. Cham: Springer, pp. 90–107.

Bowers, V. A. and Snyder, H. L., 1990, October. Concurrent versus retrospective verbal protocol for comparing window usability. *Proceedings of the Human Factors Society Annual Meeting*, 34(17): 1270–4.

Bozzon, A., Brambilla, M., Ceri, S. et al., 2013. Exploratory search framework for web data sources. *The VLDB Journal*, 22: 641–63.

Broder, A., 2002. A taxonomy of web search. *ACM Sigir Forum*, 36(2): 3–10.

Byström, K. and Järvelin, K., 1995. Task complexity affects information seeking and use. *Information Processing & Management*, 31(2): 191–213. https://doi.org/10.1016/0306-4573(95)80035-R

Cadwell, P., Castilho, S., O'Brien, S. and Mitchell, L., 2016. Human factors in machine translation and post-editing among institutional translators. *Translation Spaces*, 5(2): 222–43.

Carl, M. and Schaeffer, M., 2018. The development of the TPR-DB as grounded theory method. *Translation, Cognition & Behavior*, 1(1): 168–93.

Carl, M., Schaeffer, M. and Bangalore, S., 2016. The CRITT translation process research database. In M. Carl, S. Bangalore and M. Schaeffer (eds.) *New Directions in Empirical Translation Process Research*. Cham: Springer, pp. 13–54.

Case, D. O. and Given, L. M., 2016. *Looking for Information: A Survey of Research on Information Seeking, Needs, and Behavior*. 4th ed. Bingley: Emerald Group Publishing.

Ceri, S., Bozzon, A., Brambilla, M. et al. 2013. *Web Information Retrieval*. Heidelberg: Springer Science & Business Media.

Cho, H., Powell, D., Pichon, A. et al., 2019. Eye-tracking retrospective think-aloud as a novel approach for a usability evaluation. *International Journal of Medical Informatics*, 129: 366–73.

Conklin, K., Pellicer-Sánchez, A. and Carrol, G., 2018. *Eye-Tracking: A Guide for Applied Linguistics Research*. Cambridge: Cambridge University Press.

Costa, V., Sias Rodrigues, A., Agostini, L. B. et al., 2019. The potential of user experience (UX) as an approach of evaluation in tangible user interfaces (TUI). International Conference on Human-Computer Interaction. In A. Marcus and W. Wang (eds.) *Design, User Experience, and Usability: Practice and Case Studies*. Cham: Springer Nature, pp.30–48.

Cui, Y. and Zheng, B., 2021a. Consultation behaviour with online resources in English–Chinese translation: An eye-tracking, screen-recording and retrospective study. *Perspectives*, 29(5): 740–60.

Cui, Y. and Zheng, B., 2021b. Effect of perceived translation difficulty on the allocation of cognitive resources between translating and consultation: An eye-tracking and screen-recording study. In C. Wang and B. Zheng (eds.) *Empirical Studies of Translation and Interpreting*. London: Routledge, pp. 51–73.

Dervin, B., 1983. An overview of sense-making research: Concepts, methods and results. Paper presented at the annual meeting of the International Communication Association, Dallas, TX, May. http://communication.sbs .ohio-state.edu/sense-making/art/artdervin83.html.

Dervin, B., 1998. Sense-making theory and practice: An overview of user interests in knowledge seeking and use. *Journal of Knowledge Management*, 2(2): 36–46.

Doherty, S. and O'Brien, S., 2014. Assessing the usability of raw machine translated output: A user-centered study using eye tracking. *International Journal of Human-Computer Interaction*, 30(1): 40–51.

Ehrensberger-Dow, M. and Perrin D., 2009. Capturing translation processes to access metalinguistic awareness. *Across Languages and Cultures*, 10(2): 275–88.

EMT. 2017. EMT Competence Framework. https://ec.europa.eu/info/sites/ default/files/emt_competence_fwk_2017_en_web.pdf

Enríquez Raído, V., 2011. Investigating the Web Search Behaviors of Translation Students: An Exploratory and Multiple-Case Study. Unpublished PhD thesis. Barcelona: Universitat Ramon Llull.

Enríquez Raído, V., 2014. *Translation and Web Searching*. 1st ed. New York: Routledge.

Ericsson, K. A. and Simon, H. A., 1998. How to study thinking in everyday life: Contrasting think-aloud protocols with descriptions and explanations of thinking. *Mind, Culture, and Activity*, 5(3): 178–86.

Fidel, R., 2012. *Human Information Interaction: An Ecological Approach to Information Behavior.* Cambridge, MA: MIT Press.

Fogg, B. J., 2003, April. Prominence-interpretation theory: Explaining how people assess credibility online. In *CHI'03 Extended Abstracts on Human Factors in Computing Systems.* Gilbert Cockton (Chair). New York: Association for Computing Machinery, pp. 722–3.

Gero, J. S. and Tang, H. H., 2001. The differences between retrospective and concurrent protocols in revealing the process-oriented aspects of the design process. *Design Studies*, 22(3): 283–95.

Glenn, J.C., 2010. *Handbook of Research Methods.* Jaipur: Oxford Book Company.

Göpferich, S., 2009. Towards a model of translation competence and acquisition: The longitudinal study TransComp. In S. Göpferich, A. Lykke Jakobsen and I.M. Mees (eds.) *Behind the Mind: Methods, Models and Results in Translation Process Research.* Copenhagen: Samfundslitterature Press, pp. 11–37.

Gough, J., 2016. The Patterns of Interaction between Professional Translators and Online Resources. Unpublished PhD thesis. University of Surrey, UK.

Granka, L., Feusner, M. and Lorigo, L., 2008. Eye monitoring in online search. In R. I. Hammoud (ed.) *Passive Eye Monitoring.* Berlin: Springer, pp. 347–72.

Granka, L. A., Joachims, T. and Gay, G., 2004, July. Eye-tracking analysis of user behavior in WWW search. In *Proceedings of the 27th Annual International ACM SIGIR Conference on Research and Development in Information Retrieval.* New York: Association for Computing Machinery, pp. 478–9.

Guerberof Arenas, A., Moorkens, J. and O'Brien, S., 2021. The impact of translation modality on user experience: An eye-tracking study of the Microsoft Word user interface. *Machine Translation*, 35(2): 205–37.

Hansen, J. P., 1991. The use of eye mark recordings to support verbal retrospection in software testing. *Acta Psychologica*, 76(1): 31–49.

Hartson, H. R. and Hix, D., 1989. Human-computer interface development: Concepts and systems for its management. *ACM Computing Surveys (CSUR)*, 21(1): 5–92.

Hodkinson, C., Geoffrey, K. and Mccoll-Kennedy, J. R., 2000. Consumer web search behaviour: Diagrammatic illustration of wayfinding on the web. *International Journal of Human-Computer Studies*, 52(5): 805–30. https://doi.org/10.1006/ijhc.1999.0357

Holmqvist, K., Nyström, M., Andersson, R. et al., 2011. *Eye Tracking: A Comprehensive Guide to Methods and Measures.* Oxford: Oxford University Press.

Hvelplund, K. T., 2017. Translators' use of digital resources during translation. *HERMES – Journal of Language and Communication in Business*, 56: 71–87.

Hvelplund, K. T., 2019. Digital resources in the translation process: Attention, cognitive effort and processing flow. *Perspectives*, 27(4): 510–24.

Joachims, T., Granka, L., Pan, B. et al., 2007. Evaluating the accuracy of implicit feedback from clicks and query reformulations in web search. *ACM Transactions on Information Systems (TOIS)*, 25(2): 1–27.

Jones, W., Pirolli, P., Card, S. K. et al., 2006. It's about the information stupid! Why we need a separate field of human-information interaction. *CHI'06 Extended Abstracts on Human Factors in Computing Systems*. ACM, pp. 65–8. https://doi.org/10.1145/1125451.1125469.

Kammerer, Y. and Gerjets, P., 2012. How search engine users evaluate and select web search results: The impact of the search engine interface on credibility assessments. *Web Search Engine Research*, 4: 251–79.

Kammerer, Y. and Gerjets, P., 2014. The role of search result position and source trustworthiness in the selection of web search results when using a list or a grid interface. *International Journal of Human-Computer Interaction*, 30(3): 177–91.

Kattenbeck, M. and Elsweiler, D., 2019. Understanding credibility judgements for web search snippets. *Aslib Journal of Information Management*, 71(1): 368–91.

Kelly, G. A., 1963. *A Theory of Personality*. New York: W. W. Norton.

Kessler, S. H. and Zillich, A. F., 2019. Searching online for information about vaccination: Assessing the influence of user-specific cognitive factors using eye tracking. *Health Communication*, 34(10): 1150–8.

Khabsa, M., Crook, A., Awadallah, A. H., Zitouni, I., Anastasakos, T. and Williams, K., 2016. Learning to account for good abandonment in search success metrics. *Proceedings of the 25th ACM International Conference on Information and Knowledge Management*, Indianapolis, United States, pp. 1893–6. https://doi.org/10.1145/2983323.2983867.

Kobayashi, M. and Takeda, K., 2000. Information retrieval on the web. *ACM Computing Surveys*, 32(2): 144–73. https://doi.org/10.1145/358923.358934.

Kuhlthau, C. C., 1990. The information search process: From theory to practice. *Journal of Education for Library and Information Science*, 31(1): 72–5.

Kuhlthau, C. C., 1991. Inside the search process: Information seeking from the user's perspective. *Journal of the American Society for Information Science*, 42(5): 361–71.

Lee, K., Hoti, K., Hughes, J. D. and Emmerton, L. M., 2015. Consumer use of "Dr Google": A survey on health information-seeking behaviors and navigational needs. *Journal of Medical Internet Research*, 17(12): e288. https://doi.org/10.2196/jmir.4345.

Lewandowski, D. and Kammerer, Y., 2021. Factors influencing viewing behaviour on search engine results pages: A review of eye-tracking research. *Behaviour & Information Technology*, 40(14): 1485–515. https://doi.org/10.1080/0144929X.2020.1761450.

Li, J., Huffman, S. and Tokuda, A., 2009, July. Good abandonment in mobile and PC internet search. *Proceedings of the 32nd International ACM SIGIR Conference on Research and Development in Information Retrieval*, pp. 43–50.

Ludolph, R., Allam, A. and Schulz, P. J., 2016. Manipulating Google's knowledge graph box to counter biased information processing during an online search on vaccination: Application of a technological debiasing strategy. *Journal of Medical Internet Research*, 18(6): e137.

Marchionini, G., 2006. Exploratory search: from finding to understanding. *Communications of the ACM*, 49(4): 41–6.

Marsh, S., 1990. Human computer interaction: An operational definition. *ACM SIGCHI Bulletin*, 22(1): 16–22.

Massey, G. and Ehrensberger-Dow, M., 2011a. Investigating information literacy: A growing priority in translation studies. *Across Languages and Cultures*, 12(2): 193–211.

Massey, G. and Ehrensberger-Dow, M., 2011b. Technical and instrumental competence in the translator's workplace: Using process research to identify educational and ergonomic needs. *ILCEA Revue de l'Institut des langues et cultures d'Europe, Amérique, Afrique, Asie et Australie*, 14. https://doi.org/10.4000/ilcea.1060.

Miller, G. A., 1983. Informavores. In F. Machlup and U. Mansfield (eds.) *The Study of Information: Interdisciplinary Messages*. New York: Wiley-Interscience, pp. 111–13.

Nickerson, R. S., 1998. Confirmation bias: A ubiquitous phenomenon in many guises. *Review of General Psychology*, 2(2): 175-220.

Nielsen, C. M., Overgaard, M., Pedersen, M. B. and Stage, J., 2005. Feedback from usability evaluation to user interface design: Are usability reports any good? In M. F. Costabile and F. Paternò (eds.) *Human-Computer Interaction – INTERACT 2005. INTERACT 2005. Lecture Notes in Computer Science*, 3585. Berlin: Springer. https://doi.org/10.1007/11555261_33.

Nielsen, J., 2006. F-shaped pattern for reading web content. *Jakob Nielsen's Alertbox*. www.useit.com/alertbox/reading_pattern.html.

O'Brien, S., 2006. Eye-tracking and translation memory matches. *Perspectives*, 14(3): 185–205.

O'Brien, S., 2010. Controlled language and readability. *Translation and Cognition*, 15: 143–68.

O'Brien, S., 2012. Translation as human–computer interaction. *Translation Spaces*, 1(1): 101–22.

O'Brien, S., 2013. The borrowers: Researching the cognitive aspects of translation. *Target. International Journal of Translation Studies*, 25(1): 5–17.

Olalla-Soler, C., 2018. Using electronic information resources to solve cultural translation problems: Differences between students and professional translators. *Journal of Documentation*, 74(6): 1293–1317. https://doi.org/ 10.1108/JD-02-2018-0033.

Olalla-Soler, C., 2019. Using translation strategies to solve cultural translation problems: Differences between students and professional translators. *Perspectives*, 27(3): 367–88.

Olsen, A., Smolentzov, L. and Strandvall, T., 2010. Comparing different eye tracking cues when using the retrospective think aloud method in usability testing. *Proceedings of the HCI 2010, 24th BCS Conference on Human Computer Interaction*, Dundee, UK, 6–10 September 2010. www.scienceopen .com/document_file/6d0b8ece-b7d1-4589-ae86-c0a35f3e6ae5/ScienceOpen/ 045_Olsen.pdf.

PACTE, 2002. Exploratory tests in a study of translation competence. *Conference Interpretation and Translation*, 4(2): 41–69.

PACTE, 2011. Results of the validation of the PACTE translation competence model: Translation project and dynamic translation index. In S. O'Brien (ed.) *Cognitive Explorations of Translation*. London: Continuum, pp. 30–56.

PACTE, 2017. PACTE translation competence model: A holistic, dynamic model of translation competence. In A. Hurtado Albir (ed.) *Researching Translation Competence by PACTE Group*. Amsterdam: John Benjamins, pp. 35–41.

Pirolli, P., 2007. *Information Foraging Theory: Adaptive Interaction with Information*. Oxford: Oxford University Press.

Preece, J., Rogers, Y., Sharpe, H., Benyon, D., Holland, S. and Carey, T., 1994. *Human–Computer Interaction*. Wokingham: Addison-Wesley.

Rowlands, I., Nicholas, D., Williams, P., Huntington, P., Fieldhouse, M., Gunter, B., Withey, R., Jamali, H. R., Dobrowolski, T. and Tenopir, C., 2008. The Google generation: The information behaviour of the researcher of the future. *Aslib Proceedings*, 60(4): 290–310.

Saldanha, G. and O'Brien, S., 2014. *Research Methodologies in Translation Studies*. London: Routledge.

Savolainen, R., 2018. Berrypicking and information foraging: Comparison of two theoretical frameworks for studying exploratory search. *Journal of Information Science*, 44(5): 580–93. https://doi.org/10.1177/0165551517713168.

Savolainen, R. and Kari, J., 2006. User-defined relevance criteria in web searching. *Journal of Documentation*, 62(6): 685–707. https://doi.org/10.1108/00220410610714921.

Shih, C. Y., 2017. Web search for translation: An exploratory study on six Chinese trainee translators' behaviour. *Asia Pacific Translation and Intercultural Studies*, 4(1): 50–66. https://doi.org/10.1080/23306343.2017.1284641.

Shih, C. Y., 2019. A quest for web search optimisation: An evidence-based approach to trainee translators' behaviour Perspectives, 27(6): 908–23. https://doi.org/10.1080/0907676X.2019.1579847.

Shih, C. Y., 2021. Navigating the web: A study on professional translators' behaviour. In C. Wang and B. Zheng (eds.) *Empirical Studies of Translation and Interpreting: The Post-Structuralist Approach*. New York: Routledge, pp. 74–92.

Shih, C. Y., in press. From the periphery to the centre of investigation and beyond: affect and emotion in translation process research. In C. Shih and C. Wang (eds.) *Translation and Interpreting as Social Interaction*, London: Bloomsbury.

Shreve, G. M., 2006. The deliberate practice: Translation and expertise. *Journal of Translation Studies*, 9(1): 27–42.

Stephens, D. W. and Krebs, J. R., 1986. *Foraging Theory*. Princeton, NJ: Princeton University Press.

Spink, A. and Jansen, B. J. (eds.), 2004. *Web Search: Public Searching of the Web*. Dordrecht: Springer Netherlands.

Sycz-Opoń, J., 2019. Information-seeking behaviour of translation students at the University of Silesia during legal translation: An empirical investigation. *The Interpreter and Translator Trainer*, 13(2): 152–76.

Sycz-Opoń, J. E., 2021. Trainee translators' research styles: A taxonomy based on an observation study at the university of Silesia, Poland. *Translation & Interpreting*, 13(2): 136–63.

Tanner, S., McCarthy, M. and O'Reilly, S., 2020. Using eye-tracking and retrospective think aloud as a probing tool in food labelling research: An abstract. In F. Pantoja, S. Wu and N. Krey (eds.) *Enlightened Marketing in Challenging Times: Proceedings of the 2019 AMS World Marketing Congress (WMC)*. Cham Springer, pp. 555–6.

Van den Haak, M., De Jong, M. and Jan Schellens, P., 2003. Retrospective vs. concurrent think-aloud protocols: Testing the usability of an online library catalogue. *Behaviour & Information Technology*, 22(5): 339–51.

Van der Meer, J. and Ruopp, A., 2015. MT Market Report 2014. *TAUS – Enabling Better Translation*. www.taus.net/think-tank/reports/translate-reports/mt-market-report-2014.

Wang, J., 2018. Information seeking behaviour in two-way translation: An empirical study. Unpublished MPhil thesis. Guildford: University of Surrey.

White, R, Marchionini, G. and Muresan, G., 2008. Evaluating exploratory search systems: Introduction to special topic issue of information processing and management. *Information Processing & Management*, 44(2): 433–6.

White, R. W., 2016. *Interactions with Search Systems*. Cambridge: Cambridge University Press.

Whyatt, B., Witczak, O. and Tomczak, E., 2021. Information behaviour in bidirectional translators: Focus on online resources. *The Interpreter and Translator Trainer*, 15(2): 154–71.

Wilson, T. D., 2000. Human information behavior. *Informing Science*, 3: 49–55.

Wu, W. C. and Kelly, D., 2014. Online search stopping behaviors: An investigation of query abandonment and task stopping. *Proceedings of the American Society for Information Science and Technology*, 51(1): 1–10.

Zhang, H., 2018. Beyond query-oriented highlighting: Investigating the effect of snippet text highlighting in search user behavior. *Computational Intelligence and Neuroscience, 2018*. https://doi.org/10.1155/2018/7836969.

Cambridge Elements ≡

Translation and Interpreting

The series is edited by Kirsten Malmkjær with Sabine Braun as associate editor for Elements focusing on Interpreting.

Kirsten Malmkjær

University of Leicester

Kirsten Malmkjær is Professor Emeritus of Translation Studies at the University of Leicester. She has taught Translation Studies at the universities of Birmingham, Cambridge, Middlesex and Leicester and has written extensively on aspects of both the theory and practice of the discipline. *Translation and Creativity* (London: Routledge) was published in 2020 and *The Cambridge Handbook of Translation*, which she edited, was published in 2022. She is preparing a volume entitled *Introducing Translation* for the Cambridge Introductions to Language and Linguistics series.

Sabine Braun

University of Surrey

Sabine Braun is Professor of Translation Studies and Director of the Centre for Translation Studies at the University of Surrey. She is a world-leading expert on interpreting and on research into human and machine interaction in translation and interpreting, for example to improve access to information, media and public services for linguistic-minority populations and other groups/people in need of communication support. She has written extensively on these topics, including *Videoconference and Remote Interpreting in Criminal Proceedings*, with J. Taylor, 2012; Here or There: Research on Interpreting via Video Link, with J. Napier and R. Skinner, 2018; and *Innovation in Audio Description Research*, with K. Starr, 2020.

Editorial Board

Adriana Serban, *Université Paul Valéry*
Barbara Ahrens, *Technische Hochschule Köln*
Liu Min-Hua, *Hong Kong Baptist University*
Christine Ji, *The University of Sydney*
Jieun Lee, *Ewha Womans University*
Lorraine Leeson, *The University of Dublin*
Sara Laviosa, *Università Delgi Stuidi di Bari Aldo Moro*
Fabio Alves, *FALE-UFMG*
Moira Inghilleri, *University of Massachusetts Amherst*
Akiko Sakamoto, *University of Portsmouth*
Haidee Kotze, *Utrecht University*

About the Series

Elements in Translation and Interpreting present cutting edge studies on the theory, practice and pedagogy of translation and interpreting. The series also features work on machine learning and AI, and human-machine interaction, exploring how they relate to multilingual societies with varying communication and accessibility needs, as well as text-focused research.

Cambridge Elements ≡

Translation and Interpreting

Elements in the Series

A full series listing is available at: www.cambridge.org/EITI

Printed in the United States
by Baker & Taylor Publisher Services